ADF
1
US ARMY

OPERATION IRAQI FREEDOM
US ARMY

ABRAMS, BRADLEY & STRYKER

by Andy Renshaw and Ryan Harden

SAM PUBLICATIONS

ADF 1
Operation Iraqi Freedom – US Army: Abrams, Bradley & Stryker
by Andy Renshaw and Ryan Harden

First produced in 2010 by SAM Limited, under licence from SAM Publications
Media House, 21 Kingsway, Bedford, MK42 9BJ, United Kingdom

© 2010 SAM Publications
© Andy Renshaw and Ryan Harden – Text & Photographs
© Vincenzo Auletta – Colour Artwork
Andy Evans – Series Editor

ISBN 978-1-906959-15-9

Typeset by SAM Publications, Media House, 21 Kingsway, Bedford, MK42 9BJ, United Kingdom
Designed by Simon Sugarhood
Printed and bound in the United Kingdom by Buxton Press, United Kingdom

Acknowledgments

Andy Renshaw gives his loving appreciation to Lisa, his wife, for the understanding and encouragement to spend the countless hours needed to finish this book. Ryan Harden would also like to thank his wife Teresa and son Indy for their love and support during the production of this book.

Both authors would like to extend their thanks to the following individuals, in no particular order, who provided information, materials, and insight that helped make this title possible.

Mike Stevensen
SFC Robert Skipper '18 Bravo'
Maj. Jeff Nelson
Sgt. Pete Becerra
Hans-Hermann Bühling
MSG Jeff DeRosa
Brent Sauer
Joel Russ

Also we extend our utmost gratitude to Silvia Lo and Lucky Model and to Peter and Clair White of Creative Models, for supplying the necessary kits and paints for the model projects contained within.

www.luckymodel.com
www.creativemodels.co.uk

Andy Renshaw   Ryan Harden
April 2010

Contents

Introduction

The 2003 invasion of Iraq was led by the United States, alongside the United Kingdom and smaller contingents from Australia, Denmark and Poland. According to then President of the United States, George W. Bush and then Prime Minister of the United Kingdom, Tony Blair, the reasons for the invasion were to 'disarm Iraq of weapons of mass destruction (WMD), to end Saddam Hussein's support for terrorism, and to free the Iraqi people'. This was seen as the ultimate solution following Iraq's failure to take a 'final opportunity' to disarm itself of any alleged nuclear, chemical, and biological weapons that US and British Governments called an 'immediate and intolerable threat to world peace'.

Abrams firepower. An M1 lets rip on one of the firing ranges in Iraq

In preparation for the invasion, some 100,000 US troops were assembled in Kuwait by February 18, and at 5:34 am Baghdad time on March 20, 2003 the military invasion of Iraq began under the codename 'Operation Iraqi Liberation' later renamed 'Operation Iraqi Freedom'. Approximately forty other governments, the so-called 'coalition of the willing', also participated by providing troops, equipment, services, security, and Special Forces. The stated objectives of the invasion were: end Sadaam Hussein's regime; eliminate weapons of mass destruction; obtain intelligence on militant networks; distribute humanitarian aid; secure Iraq's petroleum infrastructure; and to assist in creating a representative government as a model for other Middle East nations. The invasion was a quick and decisive operation that although encountering some heavy resistance, was not what the US, British and other forces expected. The Iraqi regime had been prepared to fight both a conventional and irregular war at the same time, conceding territory when faced with superior conventional forces, and launching smaller scale attacks to the rear, using fighters dressed in civilian and paramilitary clothes. This achieved some temporary successes and created unexpected challenges for the invading forces, especially the US military.

The invasion was preceded by an air strike on the Iraqi Presidential Palace on 19 March 2003, and the following day coalition forces launched into Basra Province from their massing point near the Iraqi-Kuwaiti border. Meanwhile commandos launched an amphibious assault from the Persian Gulf to secure Basra and the surrounding petroleum fields, as the main invasion army moved into southern Iraq, occupying the region and engaging in the Battle of Nasiriyah on 23 March. Massive air strikes across the country and against Iraqi

A patrol group exit their Bradley IFV

command and control centres threw the defending army into chaos and prevented an effective resistance. On 26 March the 173rd Airborne Brigade was airdropped near the northern city of Kirkuk where they joined forces with Kurdish rebels and fought several actions against the Iraqi army to secure the northern part of the country, whilst the main body of coalition forces continued their drive into the heart of Iraq meeting little resistance.

Other operations occurred against pockets of the Iraqi army including the capture and occupation of Kirkuk, and the attack and capture of Tikrit. On April 9 Baghdad fell, ending President Hussein's twenty-four year rule, and US forces seized the deserted Ba'ath Party ministries and tore down a huge iron statue of Sadaam Hussein, who along with his central leadership had now gone into hiding. On 1 May a cessation of major combat operations was declared, ending the invasion stage and beginning a period of stability and rebuilding

The invasion was mercifully swift, leading to the collapse of the Iraq government and military in little under three weeks. In the aftermath of the conflict, and one of the main reasons for war, the removal of Iraq's weapons of mass destruction remains one of the most contentious issues, as although some remnants of pre-1991 production were found, it was later confirmed that these were not the weapons for which the coalition went to war. At the time of writing, security operations and work towards a democratic nation continue.

This book seeks to represent three of the United States Army's main fighting vehicles involved in the conflict: the M1 Abrams Main Battle Tank, and the M2 Bradley and Stryker Infantry Fighting Vehicles. Here you will find a background to each type, both action and walk-around reference photography and a full model build of a representative 'Iraqi Freedom' vehicle using various tools, techniques and accessories.

Andy Renshaw   Ryan Harden
April, 2010

A Stryker, covered in slat armour, a defence against RPG's, provides cover for a foot patrol on an Iraqi highway

Preparations for an invasion of Iraq were intense, and seen here US Army Strykers and Blackhawk helicopters work in concert to deploy ground troops

Glossary

AIM	Abrams Integrated Management	IFV	Infantry Fighting Vehicle
ATGM	Anti Tank Guided Missile	LRAS3	Long-Range Advanced Scout Surveillance System
BCT	Brigade Combat Team	MBT	Main Battle Tank
BUSK	Bradley Urban Survival Kit	MICV	Mechanized Infantry Combat Vehicle
CBRN	Chemical, Biological, Radiological, and Nuclear	MCLIC	Mine Clearing Line Charge
CIP	Combat Identification Panel	MGS	Mobile Gun System
CITV	Commander's Independent Thermal Viewer	NBC	Nuclear Chemical Biological
CLAW	Commander's Light Automatic Weapon	NVG	Night Vision Goggles
DVE	Driver's Vision Enhancer	ODS	Operation Desert Storm
ECM	Electronic Counter Measures	OIF	Operation Iraqi Freedom
ERA	External Reactive Armour	RPG	Rocket Propelled Grenade
FBCB2	Force XXI Battlefield Command Brigade and Below	RWS	Remote Weapons Station
FLIR	Forward Looking Infrared Radar	SBCT	Stryker Brigade Combat Team
FOB	Forward Operating Base	SEP	System Enhancement Program
GPFU	Gas Particulate Filter Units	TMS	Thermal Management System
HEAT	High Explosive Anti Tank	TOW	Tube launched Optically tracked Wire guided
HEI	High Explosive Incendiary	TUSK	Tank Urban Survival Kit
HTI	Horizontal Technology Initiative	UAAPU	Under Armor Auxiliary Power Unit
IED	Improvised Explosive Devices		

Heavily laden pair of Bradley IFV's cover a troop section in Iraq

opposite:
The business end of the 25mm M242 Bushmaster cannon. The vehicle carries 300 rounds ready and another 600 stowed in the M2, and 1,200 stowed in the M3. The ready rounds are divided between two boxes, which can be loaded with two different types of ammunition, selected on demand depending on what is needed. Both armour piercing M791 APDS-T rounds and M792 HEI-T, high explosive incendiary are available

The Abrams Main Battle Tank

Firing the main gun, a M256A1 120 mm smoothbore, a wall of flame erupts from in front of this M1A2 while at the firing range in Kuwait. The M256 is the American designation of the German Rheinmetall 120mm L44, the same gun used on the German Leopard II *(© US Army)*

Three M1A1 tanks on a test run at Camp Arifjan, Kuwait. Note that one has a dark green CIP. Stowage is almost identical on all the vehicles, even down to the box of water bottles to the left of the bustle rack APU (Auxiliary Power Unit) *(© Jeff Nelson)*

An M1A1 being positioned at a rear camp. Looking closely, the machine guns aren't mounted, smoke dischargers are covered, and the crew wears no armour vests. The extremely clean, freshly painted look may indicate that these tanks come from the Brigade Set of pre-positioned equipment that is/was located at Camp Arifjan, Kuwait. Note the unusual light green colour used on the hull *(© Jeff Nelson)*

The M1 Abrams is a third-generation main battle tank produced in the United States and named after the late General Creighton W. Abrams, who served as Army Chief of Staff and Commander of the 37th Armoured Battalion. The M1 is informally known as 'The Beast', 'Dracula' and 'Whispering Death', referring to its impressive firepower and quiet operation and is one of the heaviest tanks in service, weighing in at close to sixty-eight tons. It is a well armed, heavily armoured, and highly mobile tank designed for modern armoured ground warfare and its most notable features include the use of a powerful gas

turbine engine, the adoption of sophisticated composite armour, and separate ammunition storage in a blow-out compartment for crew safety. The M1 Abrams entered US service in 1980, replacing the 105mm gunned, fully tracked M60 Patton. It did, however, serve for over a decade alongside the improved M60A3, which had entered service in 1978. Three main versions of the M1 Abrams have so far been deployed, the M1, M1A1, and M1A2, along with various sub-variants, each incorporating improved armament, protection and electronics. These improvements, as well as periodic upgrades to older tanks, have allowed this long serving vehicle to remain in front-line action, and as such the M1A3 is currently under development and is anticipated to be in service until 2050.

The M1 Described

The first attempt to replace the aging M60 Patton was the MBT-70, developed in partnership with West Germany in the 1960's,

and this proved unsuccessful. As a result the US Army introduced the XM803 but this only succeeded in producing an expensive system with capabilities similar to the M60. Congress canceled the MBT-70 in November of 1971 and XM803 the December of the same year, and redistributed the funds to the new XM815 later renamed the XM1 Abrams. Prototypes were delivered in 1976 by Chrysler Defense and General Motors, and these came armed with a licence-built version of the 105 mm Royal Ordnance L7 gun along with a Leopard 2 for comparison. The Chrysler Defense design was later selected for development as the M1. In all some 3273 M1 Abrams were produced between 1979 and 1985 and first entered US Army service in 1980. An improved model called the M1IP was produced briefly in 1984 and contained small upgrades. Following on around 6,000 M1A1 Abrams were produced from 1986-92 and featured the M256A1 120 mm smoothbore cannon developed by Rheinmetall AG of Germany for the Leopard 2, improved armour, and a CBRN protection system.

The M256A1 main gun fires a variety of rounds, and the M829A2 was developed specifically to address the threats posed by a Soviet T-90 or T-80U tank equipped with Kontakt-5 Explosive Reactive Armour. It also fires HEAT shaped charge rounds such as the M830, the latest version of which the M830A1 incorporates a sophisticated multi-mode electronic sensing fuse and more fragmentation. The new M1028 120mm anti-personnel canister cartridge was brought into service early for use in the aftermath of the 2003 invasion of Iraq and contains 1,098 3/8-inch tungsten balls which spread from the muzzle to produce a shotgun effect, lethal out to 2,000ft. In addition to this, the new XM1111 (Mid-Range-Munition Kinetic Energy) is also in development.

A .50 cal. M2HB machine gun is also fitted in front of the

commander's hatch and on the M1, M1IP and M1A1, this gun is on a powered mount and can be fired using a 3× magnification sight, known as the 'Commander's Weapon Station' while the vehicle has all its hatches closed to protect the crew. On the M1A2 & M1A2SEP, this gun is on a flex mount, the commander having to expose himself to fire the weapon manually. The upgraded variant 'M1A1 Abrams Integrated Management' (AIM) equips the .50 caliber gun with a thermal sight for accurate night and other low-visibility shooting. An M240 7.62mm machine gun is also fitted in front of the loader's hatch on a skate mount, and a second 7.62 mm M240 machine gun in

a coaxial mount is situated to the right of the main gun. The coaxial MG is aimed and fired with the same computer fire control system used for the main gun. A further coaxial 12.7 mm M2HB machine gun can be mounted directly above the main gun in a remote weapons platform as part of the TUSK upgrade kit. The turret is also fitted with two six-barrelled smoke grenade launchers.

Armour

The Abrams is protected by the British-designed 'Chobham Armour', a further development of the British 'Burlington'

M1A1 Abrams main battle tank patrol near Tall Afar, Iraq, May 17, 2006. Looking closely the 'tan' colouring of the tank is not paint, but a solid coat of dust and mud that is covering the original three-tone scheme. Also note the lack of external stowage. Crews quickly realised the external packs, boxes, and other gear were a fire hazard if hit with RPGs. In the initial battles, many of the tanks lost were due to external fires that moved into the engine compartment
(© US Air Force, Staff Sgt Jacob N Bailey)

Abrams of Task Force 1-64 roll during the initial operations of Operation Iraqi Freedom. Note the large amount of stowed gear. The tank in the background is equipped with the TWMP, or Track Width Mine Plow which pushes aside mines buried just below the surface making a clear lane for vehicles behind it, and is one of the more favored means of mine clearing by commanders due to the speed and relative effectiveness of the technique, critical in high tempo operations
(© John Moore via Jeff Nelson)

An M1 Abrams crew from 4th Brigade, 3rd Infantry Division, awaits their turn on the firing line, at Camp Buehring, Kuwait. The encircled '68' on the front hull is a bridge weight marking, noting that this is a 68 ton vehicle. The black stripes across the turret front are Velcro (© US Army)

M1A2 system enhancement package

can impede the function of guidance systems of semi-active control line-of-sight (SACLOS) wire and radio guided anti-tank missiles and thermally and infrared guided missiles (ATGM). This device is mounted on the turret roof in front of the loader's hatch, and can lead some people to mistake Abrams fitted with these devices for the M1A2 version, since the commander's Independent Thermal Viewer on the latter is mounted in the same place, though the MCD is box-shaped and fixed in place, as opposed to cylindrical and rotating like the CITV.

The Abrams is equipped with a ballistic fire-control computer that uses 'user and system' supplied data from a variety of sources, to compute, display, and incorporate the three components of a ballistic solution – lead angle, ammunition type, and range to the target. These three components are determined using a YAG rod laser rangefinder, crosswind sensor, a pendulum static cant sensor, data concerning performance and flight characteristics of each specific type of round, tank-specific boresight alignment data, ammunition temperature, air temperature, barometric pressure, a muzzle reference system (MRS) that determines and compensates for barrel droop at the muzzle due to gravitational pull and barrel heating due to firing or sunlight, and target speed determined by tracking rate tachometers in the gunner's or commander's Control Handles. All of these factors are computed into a ballistic solution and updated thirty times per second. The updated solution is displayed in the gunner's or tank commander's field of view in the form of a reticle in both day and Thermal modes. The ballistic computer manipulates the turret and a complex arrangement of mirrors so that all one has to do is keep the reticle on the target and fire to achieve a hit. Proper lead and gun tube elevation are applied to the turret by the computer, greatly simplifying the job of the gunner.

Crew

The commander is seated to the right hand side of the turret, and his station is equipped with six periscopes which provide all round 360 degree view. The Independent Thermal Viewer from Texas Instruments provides the commander with independent stabilised day and night vision, automatic sector scanning, automatic target cueing of the gunner's sight with no need for

armour. Chobham is a composite armour formed by spacing multiple layers of various alloys of steel, ceramics, plastic composites, and Kevlar, giving greater protection from HEAT (and other chemical energy rounds) and other kinetic energy penetrators. The first M1A1 tanks to receive this upgrade were those stationed in Germany and the M1A2 tanks have now uniformly incorporated depleted uranium armour, and all M1A1 tanks in active service have been upgraded to this standard. Abrams tanks have survived multiple hits at relatively close ranges from Iraqi Lion of Babylon tanks and ATGMs, thanks to this protection. In addition to the advanced armour, some Abrams are equipped with a Missile Countermeasure Device that

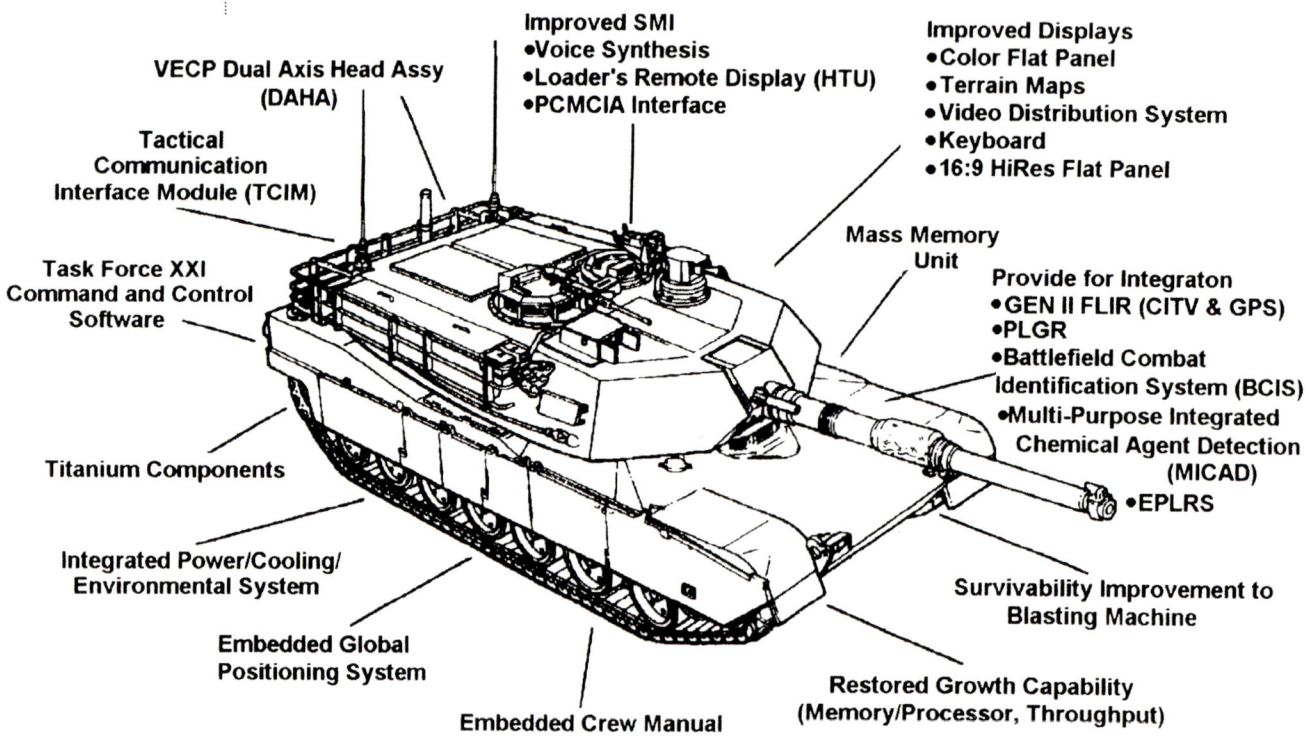

Improved SMI
•Voice Synthesis
•Loader's Remote Display (HTU)
•PCMCIA Interface

VECP Dual Axis Head Assy (DAHA)

Tactical Communication Interface Module (TCIM)

Task Force XXI Command and Control Software

Titanium Components

Integrated Power/Cooling/ Environmental System

Embedded Global Positioning System

Embedded Crew Manual

Improved Displays
•Color Flat Panel
•Terrain Maps
•Video Distribution System
•Keyboard
•16:9 HiRes Flat Panel

Mass Memory Unit

Provide for Integraton
•GEN II FLIR (CITV & GPS)
•PLGR
•Battlefield Combat Identification System (BCIS)
•Multi-Purpose Integrated Chemical Agent Detection (MICAD)
•EPLRS

Survivability Improvement to Blasting Machine

Restored Growth Capability (Memory/Processor, Throughput)

Maintenance on the turret systems gets done on 'Aphrodisiac'. Note the mix of green and tan parts, including the inside of the commander's hatch, which is dark green, showing this tank to be possibly repainted from a NATO scheme *(© US Army)*

Solders use a M88 to hoist the power-pack of this M1A1. In the background can be seen the armoured turrets of uparmoured Humvees, and the long Rhino ECM antennas. The M1 Abrams is powered by a 1,500 horsepower (1,100 kW) Honeywell AGT 1500 gas turbine *(© US Army, Spc Cynthia Teears)*

A good look at the AGT 1500 engine. This coupled with the Allison X-1100-3B Hydro-Kinetic automatic transmission gives the Abrams a governed speed of 45mph. A true 'flex-fuel' vehicle, it can run on JP-4 or JP-8 jet fuel, kerosene, diesel fuel, or any grade of gasoline. Recently the US Army selected Honeywell International Engines and Systems and General Electric to develop a new LV100-5 gas turbine engine for the M1A2. The new engine is lighter and smaller with rapid acceleration, quieter running and no visible exhaust *(© US Army, Mathew Scalise)*

As in any vehicle, a good source of air for the combustion engine is a must, and air filters are a routine maintenance point. Here a crewman beats the sand and dust from the pre-filter. Constant preventive maintenance is the way of life for the armoured vehicle crew, which keeps their machine operating and includes constant fluid checks, hub oil level checks, and inspection of the suspension for debris and damage *(© US Army)*

Other ammunition besides sabot rounds is available, including M830 HEAT (High Explosive Anti-Tank), and the new M1028 120mm anti-personnel canister cartridge. This round contains over 1,000 tungsten balls that have a shotgun effect at longer ranges, and are highly effective in making man-size holes in walls or knocking them down completely at short ranges. A semi-guided anti-tank round is also being developed for extended ranges *(© Jeff Nelson)*

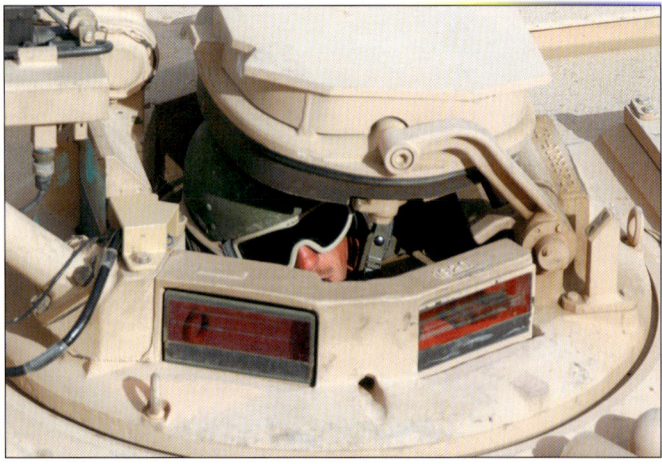

The tank commander peers from under the hatch of a M1A1. The hatch locks in three positions, including this one which provides some ventilation without completely exposing the commander. Note the casting numbers, colour of the vision blocks, and the lack of chips and scratches in the paint. CARC paint is very robust and does not chip easily (© US Army)

A peak from the loader's station into the tank commanders (TC) station. This is inside a M1A1 as note the lack of many digital features that the M1A2 has. The gunner sits in the lower half of the turret. He is only wearing the inner liner with earphones of his CVC helmet, and not the Kevlar outer shell (© US Army)

A view of the loader pushing a round into the breech. The Abrams does not have an autoloader because it's felt that manually loading is more reliable, plus it allows for the ammunition to be stored separated from the crew. A automatic power door separates the ammunition compartment from the crew, and if the ammunition ignites, the resulting explosion is directed up and out of the turret via blast panels located on top of the turret. Halon systems also engage putting out any fire within milliseconds and allow the crew to escape (© USMC)

A muddy, dirty Abrams moves down a road in the Al Boetha District in Baghdad while supporting soldiers from 5th Battalion, 20th Infantry Regiment, attached to the 2nd Brigade Combat Team, 1st Cavalry Division. The Abrams carries a spare sprocket ring and only a few necessary external stowage items including a fire blanket and traffic cones. It appears to be a M1A2 due to the lack of external APU and the shape of the TC hatch (© US Army)

Another M1A1 with the TUSK upgrade. Again note the lack of large amounts of stowed gear on the outside. One item that does seem to be consistent is a cooler, no doubt storing water (© US Army)

verbal communication, and back-up fire control. The driver's station is situated at the center front of the vehicle and is equipped with a monitoring panel showing the condition of vehicle fluid levels, batteries and electrical equipment. The driver has either three observation periscopes or two periscopes on either side, and a central image intensifying periscope for night vision. The gunner is seated on the right hand side of the turret and uses the Primary Sight-Line of Sight, GPS-LOS with a single axis stabilized head mirror. The system has daylight optics with x10 magnification narrow field of view and x3 magnification wide field of view, and unity magnification close-in surveillance with eighteen degrees field of view. The night vision Thermal Imaging System, 'TIS' has magnification x10 narrow field of view and x3 magnification wide field of view. The thermal image is displayed in the eyepiece of the gunner's sight together with the range measurement from the laser range finder. The M1A2 Abrams tank has a two-axis GPS-LOS which significantly increases the first round hit probability by providing faster target acquisition and improved gun pointing. The loader is ideally positioned both to observe around the tank and to monitor the tank's digital displays. He is responsible for the main gun and the coaxial machine gun ready box and also aims and fires the loader's machine gun. Before engagement actions are initiated, the loader searches for targets and acts as air or anti-tank guided missile guard.

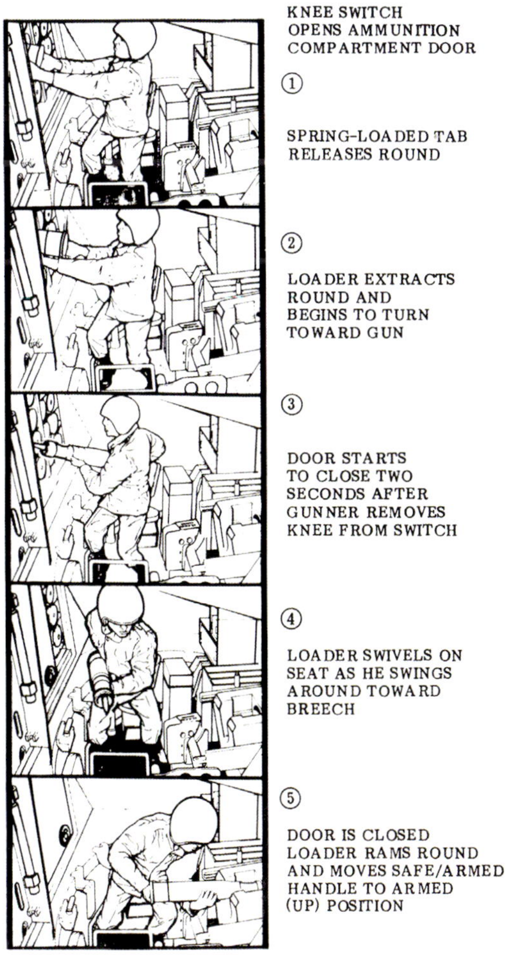

Engine

The Abrams is powered by a 1,500 horsepower Honeywell AGT 1500 gas turbine, and a six speed Allison X-1100-3B Hydro-Kinetic automatic transmission, giving it a governed top speed of 45 mph on paved roads, and 30 mph cross-country. The tank can be fuelled with diesel fuel, kerosene, any grade of motor gasoline, JP-4 jet fuel, or JP-8 jet fuel; the US Army uses JP-8 jet fuel in order to simplify logistics.

KNEE SWITCH
OPENS AMMUNITION
COMPARTMENT DOOR

SPRING-LOADED TAB
RELEASES ROUND

②

LOADER EXTRACTS
ROUND AND
BEGINS TO TURN
TOWARD GUN

③

DOOR STARTS
TO CLOSE TWO
SECONDS AFTER
GUNNER REMOVES
KNEE FROM SWITCH

④

LOADER SWIVELS ON
SEAT AS HE SWINGS
AROUND TOWARD
BREECH

⑤

DOOR IS CLOSED
LOADER RAMS ROUND
AND MOVES SAFE/ARMED
HANDLE TO ARMED
(UP) POSITION

An M1A2 and a M2A2 Bradley from 'Thunder' squadron, 3rd Armoured Cavalry Regiment, support engineers as they clear roadways of obstacles and roadblocks in Mosul, Iraq, Dec 13 2007 (© US Army)

M1A1 from the 1st Combined Arms Battalion, 63rd Armour Regiment fires at a range in Kuwait. Continual development of sabot and other munitions for the 120mm gun insure that the Abrams will remain lethal against all types of current armour. This particular M1A1 is also painted in the three-tone NATO scheme. Not all OIF tanks are tan
(© US Army, Sgt Brian Tierce)

This rather plain looking M1A2 moves through an Iraqi neighborhood. Clearly seen are the distinguishing features of the A2 including the CITV, revised commander's turret hatch, and on later models the lack of a bustle rack APU due to there being an 'under armour' APU installed within the hull *(© US Army)*

Abrams tanks from 1st Battalion, 5th Cavalry Regiment, provide overwatch for soldiers from Company B, 2nd Battalion, 12th Infantry Regiment, attached to the 1st Cavalry Division's 2nd Brigade Combat Team, while on patrol in the Al Doura district of Baghdad *(© US Army)*

TUSK

The Tank Urban Survival Kit, or 'TUSK', is a series of enhancements to the M1 Abrams intended to improve fighting ability in urban environments. Historically, urban and other close battlefields have been the worst place for tanks to fight, as their frontal armour is much stronger than that on the sides, top, or rear, and in an urban environment, attacks can come from any direction, and attackers can get close enough to reliably hit weak points in the tank's armour, or get sufficient elevation to hit the top armour square on. The TUSK system is a field installable kit that allows tanks to be upgraded without needing to be recalled to a maintenance depot. The TUSK kit includes armour upgrades to the rear and bottom of the hull, the installation of slat armour to protect the engine compartment and use of appliqué reactive armour tiles to improve flank protection. A CROWS remote controlled weapon station (RWS) mounting a .50 caliber machine gun is also now replacing the 'commander's cupola mounted heavy machine gun' on the M1A2 TUSK sets.

The TUSK kit also includes a bolt-on armoured gun shield

attached to the M240 external machine gun, which will help to protect the loader when he is in the open-hatch firing position, thus the loader will be able to use the weapon from inside, aiming it via a thermal sight which projects the target image into a pair of goggles.

The M1A2 SEP

The M1A2 SEP (System Enhancement Program), is the digital battlefield centerpiece for Army XXI. It is the heavy force vehicle that will lead Armour into the next century and transition the close combat mission to the Future Combat System (FCS). The SEP upgrade includes improved processors, colour and high resolution flat panel displays, increased memory capacity, user friendly Soldier Machine Interface (SMI) and an open operating system that will allow for future growth. Major improvements include the integration of the Second Generation Forward Looking Infra-Red (2nd Gen FLIR) sight, the Under Armour Auxiliary Power Unit (UAAPU) and a Thermal Management System (TMS).The 2nd Generation Forward Looking Infra-Red sighting system (2nd Gen FLIR) will replace the existing Thermal Image System (TIS) and the Commander's Independent Thermal Viewer. The incorporation of 2nd Gen FLIR into the M1A2 tank requires the replacement of all 1st Gen FLIR components and is seen as one of the key improvements on the SEP. The 2nd Gen FLIR is a fully integrated engagement-sighting system designed to provide the gunner and tank commander with significantly improved day and night target acquisition and engagement capability. This

Late day shot of a M1A2 SEP Abrams Tank from Troop G, 2nd Squadron, 3rd Armoured Cavalry Regiment outside of Muqdadiyah, Iraq. This tank is equipped with a Rhino ECM antenna and what appears to be a backboard lashed to the turret side (© US Army)

system allows 70% better acquisition, 45% quicker firing and greater accuracy. In addition, a gain of 30% greater range for target acquisition and identification will increase lethality and lessen fratricide. The Commander's Independent Thermal Viewer (CITV) provides a hunter-killer capability. The 2nd GEN FLIR is a variable power sighting system ranging from three or six power (wide field of view) for target acquisition and thirteen, twenty-five or fifty power (narrow field of view) for engaging targets at appropriate range.

Abrams at War

The Abrams remained untested in combat until the Gulf War in 1991 when a total of 1,848 M1A1s were deployed to Saudi Arabia. The M1A1 was superior to Iraq's Soviet-era T-55 and T-62 tanks, as well as Iraqi assembled Russian T-72s, and locally-produced copies, the 'Asad Babil'. The M1A2 was a further

These M1A1s belong to 1st Platoon, Delta Company, 2nd Combined Arms Battalion, 69th Armour Regiment and arc outfitted with the Tank Urban Survivability Kit (TUSK). This upgrade came from the result of early OIF experience that showed the vulnerability of the Abrams to RPG attacks by infantry in close quarters. The ERA blocks provide a layer of protection while the armoured shields and weapons give the crew a better chance of defending from aggressors on foot (© US Army)

A M1A1 TUSK conducts a counter improvised explosive device mission in Baghdad, Iraq, Dec. 22, 2007. The combination of warning signs, debris, and overhead directional signs would make this a unique diorama for a modeler wanting to place their Abrams is a slightly different setting
(© US Army, Spc Luke Thornberry)

Looking through the razor wire, tankers roll back out on patrol after refuelling at Joint Security Station Sadr in Baghdad, April 4, 2008. Again note the lack of much gear stowed on the outside and relative lack of markings
(© US Army)

'Bad Blood', a M1A1 TUSK from Bravo Company, 1st BN, 35th Armoured Regiment, 2nd BCT, 1st Armoured Division, at Al-Rahman, Iraq, shows some interesting features. Note the extra armoured cupola around the tank commander's station. Improvements and upgrades were fielded as soon as available, and were usually installable by unit crews, so it's not uncommon to see a mix of features from various TUSK and other upgrade **programs** *(© US Army, Spc Chase Kincaid)*

An up-close shot of the side of 'Bad Blood'. There is a 'slave' cable wrapped around the smoke discharger, spare road wheel and track segment, plus a rusty exhaust deflector. The heat from the turbine exhaust would quickly degrade the metal to where the slightest moisture would cause rust. It is meant to be installed on the rear exhaust grill and keeps infantry from being hit with the turbine blast *(© US Army, Spc Chase Kincaid)*

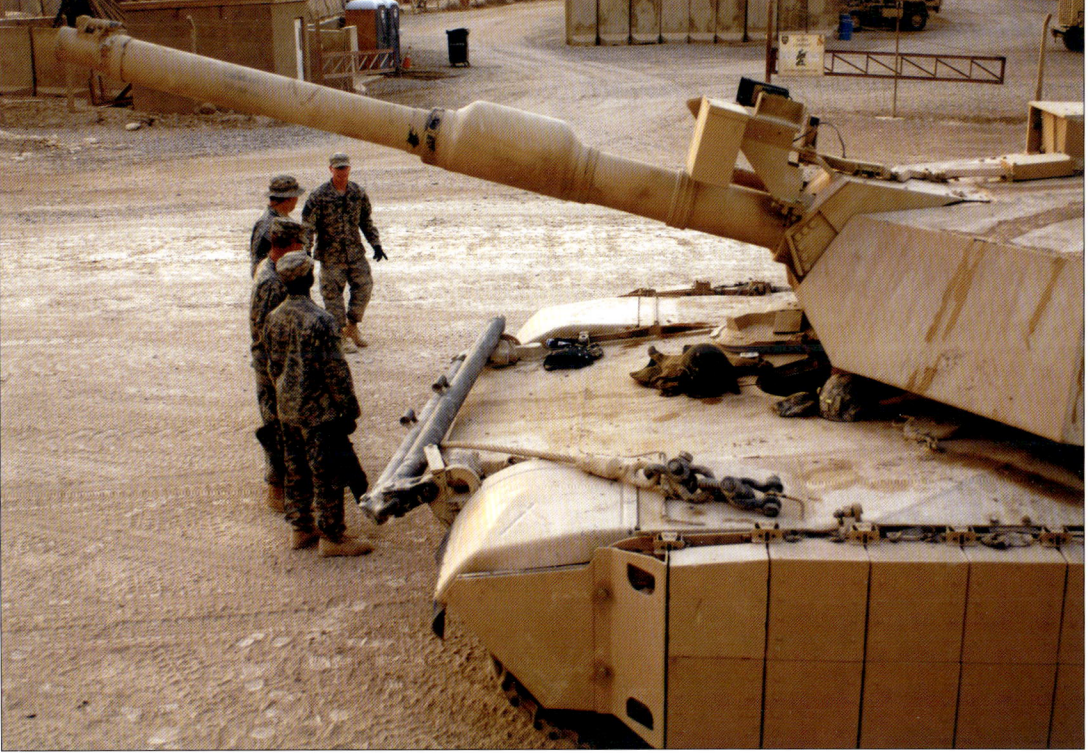

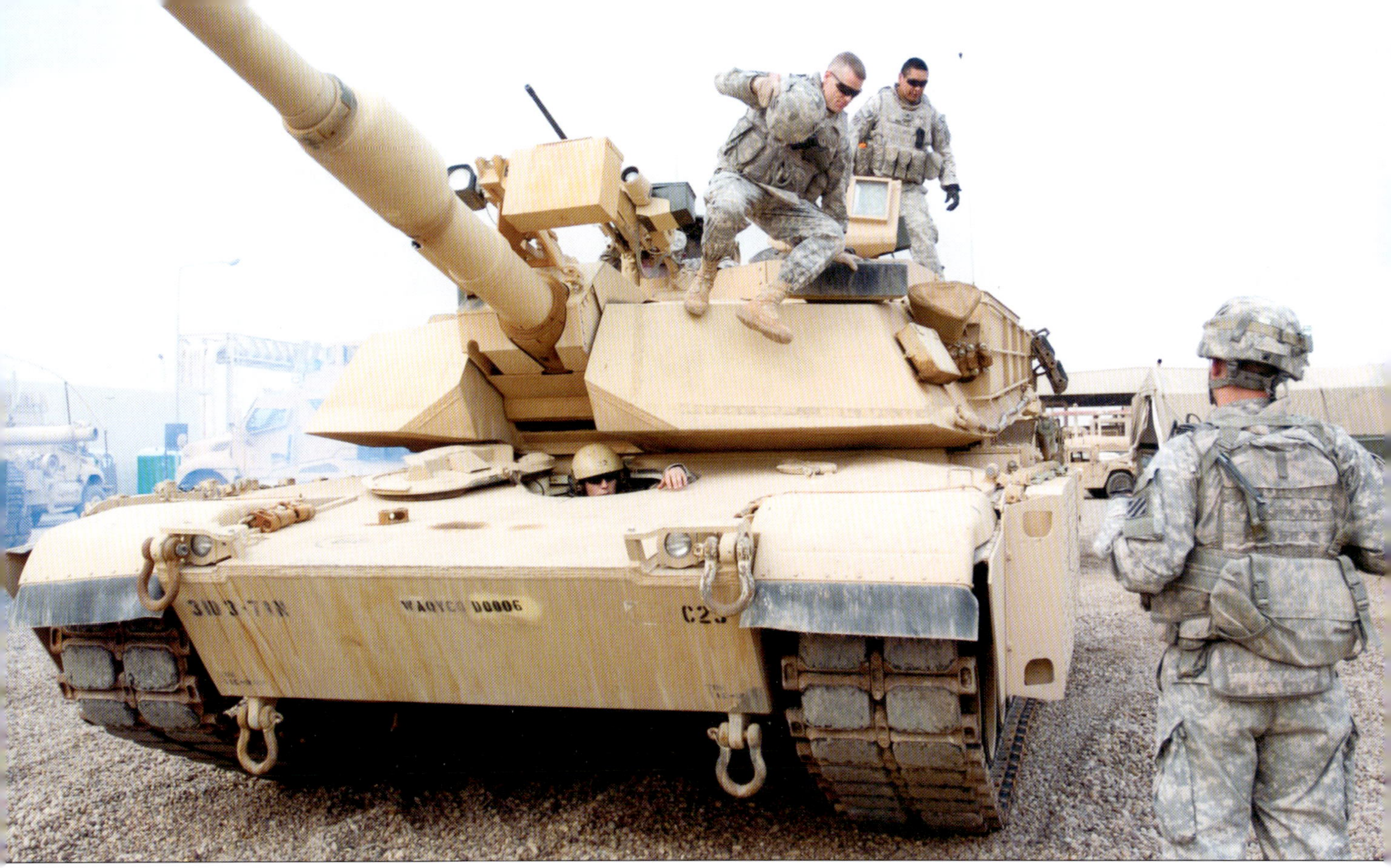

This particular shot is a great colour reference not just for the paint on the hull itself, but also the colour of the track
(© US Army)

U.S. Army Soldiers assigned to 1st Platoon, Delta Company, 2nd Combined Arms Battalion, 69th Armour Regiment prepare an M1A1 Abrams for a patrol along a supply route. The staining on the turret and overall grimy appearance should be of interest of those wanting to do realistic weathering to their Abrams models
(© US Army)

improvement of the M1A1 with a commander's independent thermal viewer and weapon station, position navigation equipment, digital data bus and a radio interface unit. The M1A2 SEP (System Enhancement Package) added digital maps, FBCB2 (Force XXI Battlefield Command Brigade and Below) capabilities, and an improved cooling system to maintain crew compartment temperature with the addition of multiple computer systems to the M1A2 tank. Further upgrades included depleted uranium armour for all variants, a system overhaul that returns all A1s to like-new condition (M1A1 AIM), a digital enhancement package for the A1 (M1A1D), a commonality program to standardise parts between the US Army and the Marine Corps (M1A1HC) and an electronic upgrade for the A2 (M1A2 SEP). During Operations Desert Shield and Desert Storm and in Bosnia, some M1A1s were modified with the armour upgrades described earlier and additionally the M1 can be equipped with mine plow and mine roller attachments if needed. The M1 chassis also serves as a basis for the 'Grizzly' combat engineering vehicle and the M104 Wolverine heavy assault bridge.

During Operation Iraqi Freedom in 2003, M1's were again in the thick of the action and were also outfitted with new 'Combat Identification Panels' to reduce the chance of friendly fire incidents. These panels were mounted on the sides and rear of

A pair of Abrams roll through streets on urban patrol. The US Army is looking to keep the Abrams for several more decades, and continual upgrades and improvements will ensure it continues to protect its crew and be lethal on the battlefield *(© US Army)*

Iraqi traffic patrol! *(© US Army)*

Either dusk or early dawn, this M1A1 patrols a highway. The spotlight on the barrel-mounted 50 cal M2HB machine gun is on. In many cases, the sheer presence of heavy armour acts as a strong deterrent to insurgents planting roadside bombs or mounting attacks *(© US Army)*

A U.S. M1A1 Abrams tank, from Bravo Company, 1st Battalion, 35th Armoured Regiment, 2nd Brigade Combat Team, 1st Armoured Division, uses mine rollers to clear a field of pressure plate landmines, at Al-Rahman, Iraq, Dec 2008 *(© US Army, Spc Chase Kincaid)*

Soldiers from 1st Combined Arms Battalion, 68th Armour Regiment, 3rd Brigade Combat Team, 4th Infantry Division, Multi-National Division – Baghdad, manoeuvre an M1A2 Abrams tank as they return to Combat Outpost Ford, April 9, after a mission in northern Baghdad (© US Army)

A great shot showing the details of the barrel-mounted M2HB 50 cal machine gun. Note the tank in the background has several extra spotlights mounted (© US Army)

Frontal shot of Bad Blood. The 'Mine Clearing Roller', or MCR is used to detonate pressure mines thus clearing a 3.6ft (1.1m) path in front of each track. It is best used to proof lanes already cleared by other means, such as the MCB or MICLIC (© US Army, Spc Chase Kincaid)

'Bad Blood' gets a workout clearing mines. During operations, the turret is turned to the side to protect the barrel from any explosion resulting from detonating a mine (© US Army, Spc Chase Kincaid)

A low angle shot of an M1 showing the underside of the mine plow (© US Army)

'Blood and Guts', a M1A2 shows off a short lived part of the TUSK upgrade program which was a small section of slat armour added behind the engine to protect this area from RPG attack. It was found to be cumbersome to work around and by the time it was introduced the RPG threat had diminished (© LTC(Ret) Timothy Webb)

the turret, shaped as a 'four-cornered 'box'. Some Abrams were also fitted with a secondary storage bin on the back of the existing bustle rack to the rear of the turret, often referred to as a 'bustle rack extension' to enable the crew to carry more supplies and personal belongings. Some Abrams were disabled by Iraqi infantrymen in ambushes during the invasion, employing short-range anti-tank rockets fired at the tracks, rear and top of the vehicles. Others were put out of action when struck in critical places by heavy calibre machine gun rounds. No Abrams crew member was lost to hostile fire during the initial invasion of Iraq, although several tank crew members were later killed by snipers and roadside bombs during the occupation that followed. However, in October 2003, two soldiers were killed and a third wounded when their tank was disabled by an anti-tank mine, which was combined with 1,100 lb of other explosives including several 155 mm rounds to increase its effect. The massive explosion beneath the tank knocked off the turret and marked the first time deaths had resulted from a hostile-fire assault on the M1 tank from enemy forces. The most one-sided engagement of the war came when M1A2s destroyed seven T-72 'Lion of Babylon' tanks in a point-blank skirmish near Mahmoudiyah, some eighteen miles south of Baghdad. In addition to the Abrams' already heavy armament, some crews were also issued M136 AT4 shoulder-fired anti-tank weapons under the assumption that they might have to engage heavy armor in tight urban areas where the main gun couldn't be brought to bear. During an early attack on Baghdad, one M1A1 was disabled by a recoilless rifle round that had penetrated the

Another shot of the 68th AR M1A2s returning to Combat Outpost Ford. The barrel-mounted M2HB is not mounted. This also gives a glimpse of the additional armour plating that was added to the bottom of the hull. The plating is in the shape of a shallow 'V' to help deflect some of the blast from a mine or IED *(© US Army)*

rear engine housing, and punctured a hole in the right rear fuel cell, causing fuel to leak onto the hot turbine engine. After repeated attempts to extinguish the fire, the decision was made to destroy or remove any sensitive equipment. Oil and .50 calibre rounds were scattered in the interior, the ammunition doors were opened and several Thermite grenades ignited inside. Another M1 then fired a HEAT round in order to ensure its destruction. Although the tank was rendered unusable, it was still intact! Later, an AGM-65 Maverick and two AGM-114 Hellfire missiles were fired into the vehicle to complete its destruction. Due to the vulnerability of tanks in urban combat, the Tank Urban Survival Kit, or TUSK (described earlier), was developed and issued to M1 units.

M1 VARIANTS	
XM1	Experimental model. Nine test-beds were produced in 1978
M1	First production variant. Production began in 1979 and continued to 1985
M1IP	Improvement Production: Produced briefly in 1984 before the M1A1, contained upgrades and reconfigurations
M1A1	Production started in 1986 and continued to 1992 (4,976 built for the US Army, 221 for USMC, 755 for Egypt, 59 M1A1 AIM SA sold to Australia)
M1A1HC	Heavy Common: Added new depleted uranium armour mesh, pressurised NBC system, rear bustle rack for improved stowage and M256 120 mm smoothbore cannon
M1A1-D	Digital: A digital upgrade for the M1A1HC, to keep up with M1A2 SEP
M1A1-AIM	Abrams Integrated Management: A program whereby older tanks are reconditioned to zero-hour and tank improved by adding a Forward-Looking Infra-Red (FLIR), Far Target Locate sensors, a tank-infantry phone, communications gear, including FBCB2 and Blue Force Tracking, and a thermal sight for the .50 caliber machine gun
M1A1 KVT	Krasnovian Variant Tank: M1A1s that have been visually modified to resemble Soviet-made tanks for use at the National Training Center, fitted with MILES gear and a Hoffman device
M1A1M	An export variant ordered by the Iraqi Army
M1A2	Baseline: Production began in 1992 (77 built for the US and more than 600 M1s upgraded to M1A2, 315 for Saudi Arabia, 218 for Kuwait). The M1A2 offers the tank commander an independent thermal sight and ability to, in rapid sequence; shoot at two targets without the need to acquire each one sequentially
M1A2 SEP	System Enhancement Package: Has upgraded 3rd generation depleted uranium encased armour with graphite coating (240 new built, 300 M1A2s upgraded to M1A2 SEP for the USA, 250 for Egypt
M1 Grizzly Combat Mobility Vehicle (CMV)	
M1 Panther II Remote Controlled Mine Clearing Vehicle	
M104 Wolverine Heavy Assault Bridge	
M1 Panther II Mine Clearing Blade/Roller System.	
M1 Assault Breacher Vehicle Assault variant for the USMC	

Abrams Walkaround

Port side mountings for the TUSK reactive armour *(© MSG Jeff DeRosa)*

Starboard side mountings for the TUSK reactive armour *(© MSG Jeff DeRosa)*

Explosive Reactive Tiles, part of the TUSK upgrade fitted to the flanks of the Abrams
(© MSG Jeff DeRosa)

Rear aspect of the turret showing stowage *(© MSG Jeff DeRosa)*

Close-up beneath the gun installation *(© MSG Jeff DeRosa)*

Rear aspect showing grilles *(© MSG Jeff DeRosa)*

The main armament of the M1A1 and M1A2 is the M256A1 120 mm smoothbore gun
(© MSG Jeff DeRosa)

A .50 cal. (M2HB machine gun in front of the commander's hatch with its 3× magnification sight, known as the Commander's Weapon Station (CWS)
(© MSG Jeff DeRosa)

The Abrams is equipped with a ballistic fire-control computer that uses user and system-supplied data from a variety of sources
(© MSG Jeff DeRosa)

Undergoing maintenance at Camp Arifjan, Kuwait. This M1A1 Abrams Tank from the 1st Combined Arms Battalion, 63rd Armour Regiment, 2nd Brigade, 1st Infantry Division gives us a good look of a TUSK tank without the ERA blocks attached
(© US Army, Sgt Brian Tierce)

A good view of the external kit stowed on the Abrams
(© Brent Sauer)

The M1 Abrams is powered by a 1,500 horsepower (1,100 kW) Honeywell AGT 1500 gas turbine, and a six speed (four forward, two reverse) Allison X-1100-3B Hydro-Kinetic automatic transmission, giving it a governed top speed of 45 mph

Wheels in detail *(© Brent Sauer)*

Forward plow undergoing recovery maintenance *(© Brent Sauer)*

Obviously at a rear camp due to the lack of personal armoured vests and helmet, this M1A1 crew load sabot 120mm ammunition, the M829A2 APFSDS-T (Armour Piercing, Fin Stabilized Discarding Sabot and Tracer). When fired, the round sheds its outer casing leaving the long pointed rod which is made of depleted uranium (DU) and which punctures its way through armour using kinetic energy. The resulting penetration combined with fragments of the armour and penetrator, plus melted elements from the heat of the penetration, ricochet inside the tank with devastating results *(© US Army)*

Frontal plow in detail
(© Brent Sauer)

A heavily stowed Abrams! *(© Brent Sauer)*

A second 7.62 mm M240 machine gun in a coaxial mount to the right of the main gun
(© Brent Sauer)

The turret is fitted with two six-barrelled smoke grenade launchers *(© Brent Sauer)*

Stowage on the rear of the turret *(© Brent Sauer)*

Vision blocks *(© Brent Sauer)*

1 Abrams Profiles

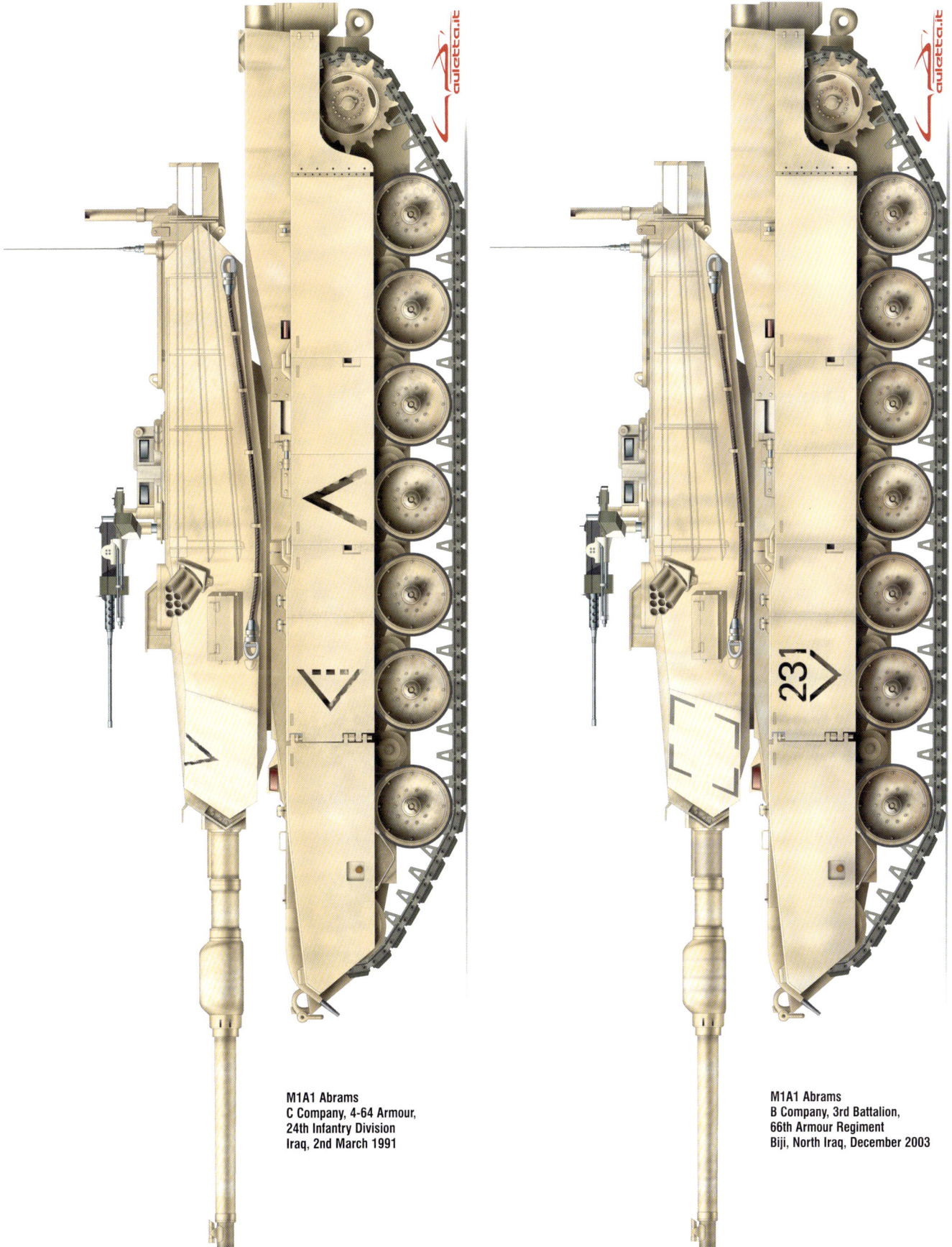

M1A1 Abrams
C Company, 4-64 Armour,
24th Infantry Division
Iraq, 2nd March 1991

M1A1 Abrams
B Company, 3rd Battalion,
66th Armour Regiment
Biji, North Iraq, December 2003

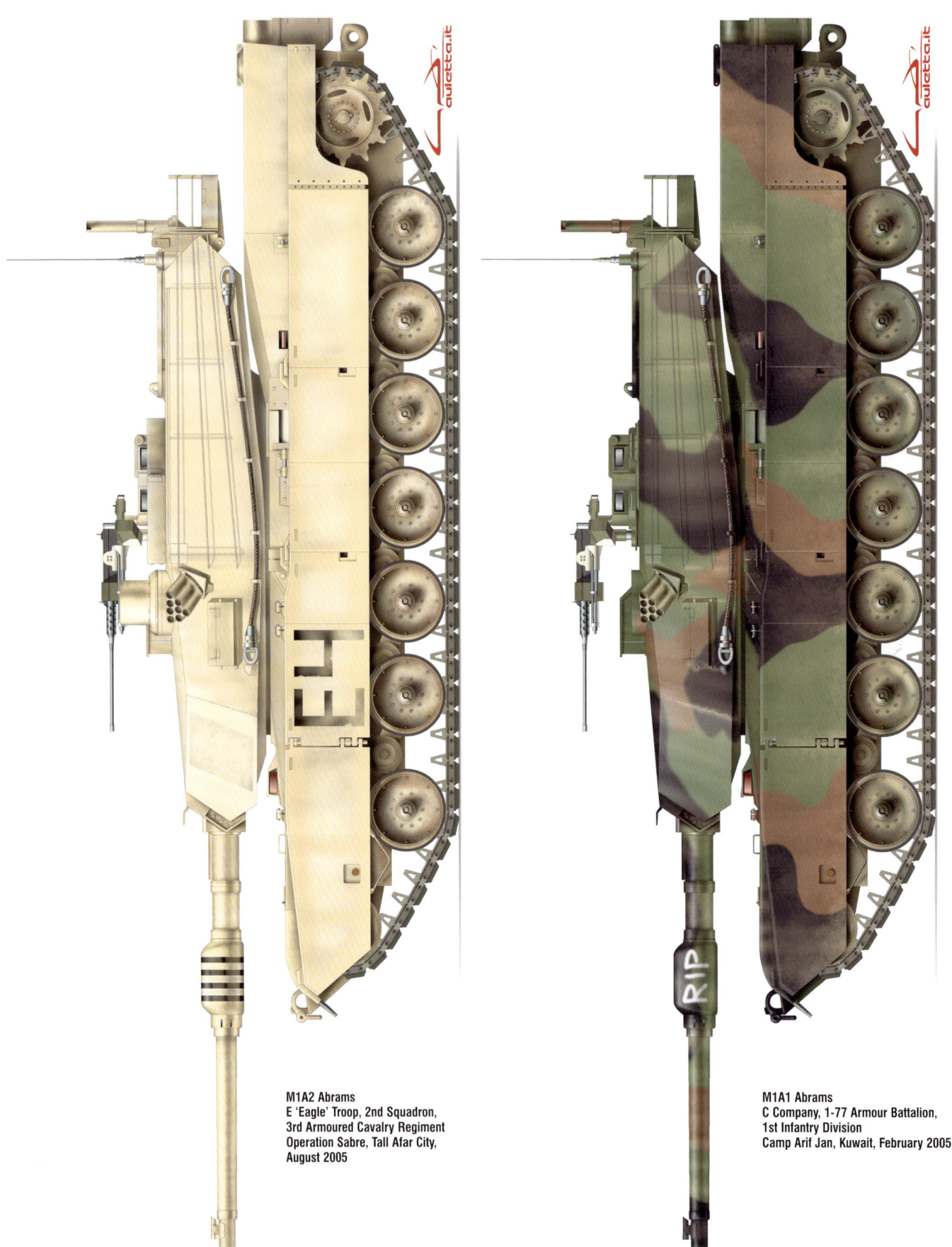

M1A2 Abrams
E 'Eagle' Troop, 2nd Squadron,
3rd Armoured Cavalry Regiment
Operation Sabre, Tall Afar City,
August 2005

M1A1 Abrams
C Company, 1-77 Armour Battalion,
1st Infantry Division
Camp Arif Jan, Kuwait, February 2005

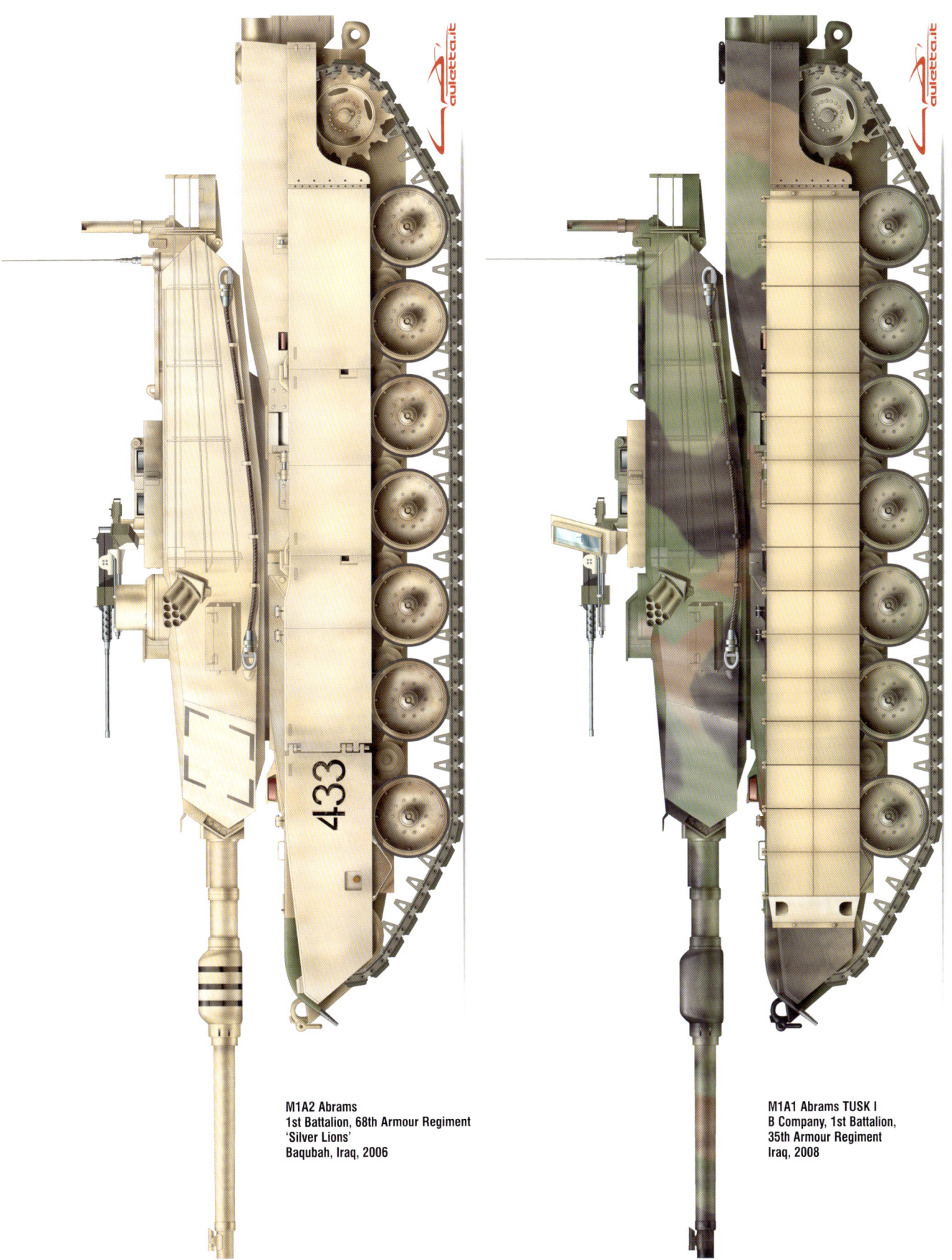

M1A2 Abrams
1st Battalion, 68th Armour Regiment
'Silver Lions'
Baqubah, Iraq, 2006

M1A1 Abrams TUSK I
B Company, 1st Battalion,
35th Armour Regiment
Iraq, 2008

1 Modelling the Abrams M1A2 TUSK

Ryan Harden

Although not the most accurate scale model of the Abrams on the market, for this project it made sense to use the 1:35 Tamiya M1A2 kit, combined with the Legend Productions resin Abrams TUSK, upgrade set, Voyager's Slat Armour and copious amounts of Eduard etch. This method was chosen for two reasons, firstly to demonstrate what can be achieved from a perceived 'simpler kit', with a low part-count and an easier assembly than say the Dragon Abrams, with its larger number of parts and greater difficulty level, and secondly it allowed me let me more time to spend with the resin and etch parts.

The Legend set is very comprehensive, but the instructions are a little sparse, being no more than a series of photos of the

The blank canvas! The Tamiya 1:35 scale M1A2 Abrams. While the kit has a mix of original and new tooling parts, it is the perfect starting point for this build

assembled conversion. So good reference material is a must when attempting this type of work, as the manufacturer's instructions may not tell the whole story when it comes to the placement of some of the parts. On first inspection the cream coloured resin on some of the finer details had cured to a clear colour giving the illusion that the parts were not completely moulded. A primer coat revealed another story however, and all were perfectly formed with crisp detail. Resin is very susceptible to heat and some of the parts were warped, but nothing a hair dryer could not coax back into shape. The skirt resin was so sensitive to temperature in fact, that even late in the build I could almost give a weather forecast depending on the splay of the parts!

Voyager's rear Slat Armour had to be added to the model; although current TUSK Abrams units do not use this feature

any more, it just looked so cool in some of my references; I just had to add it. Although this set was designed to fit the Dragon Abrams, it was 'shimmed-up' to fit the wider Tamiya rear end. Both The Eduard and Voyager brass sets were assembled with the help of the Mission Models Etch Mate, a product well worth the small investment as it really gives control when folding the parts in preparation for the glue.

Careful thought on how you will complete the build and the painting sequence is a must before finalising the build. Most of the resin parts fit very well, but you will still need to dry fit these to be sure. Thinking ahead to the painting sequence, I decided to build some parts as smaller sub-assemblies rather than assembling the whole tank and then begin painting. The skirts are a good example of this method.

The Abrams I am depicting in this build carried no markings, in fact most of the reference shots show unit numbers oversprayed in the field. The model was not intended to represent a specific vehicle, more a generic tank with features pulled from different reference sources. To that end the Tankograd book on the subject was invaluable to completing the project; however the Internet and other sources were used to check on specific details. I would be the first to agree this build is not the most accurate in the world; however, it was designed to show – as described earlier, what can be achieved by modellers of all skill levels. This is therefore what you could describe as a building block, and can be taken even further if you so desire.

The approach I use to painting is simple, airbrush as much as possible! Even if the temptation is there to quickly brush paint a part or surface there is, in my opinion, no substitute for a finely airbrushed finish. Of course there are some

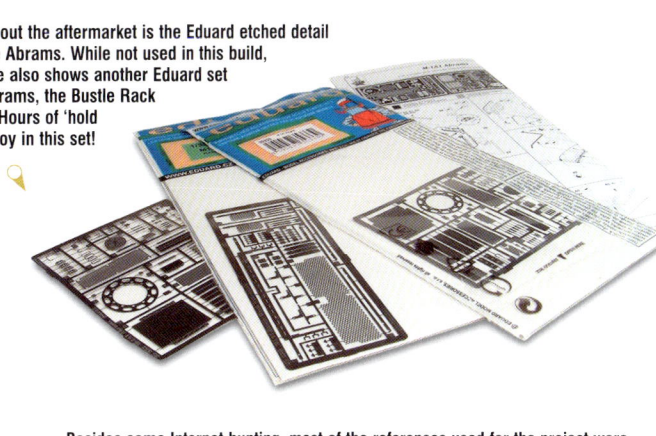

Rounding out the aftermarket is the Eduard etched detail set for the Abrams. While not used in this build, the picture also shows another Eduard set for the Abrams, the Bustle Rack extender. Hours of 'hold and fold' joy in this set!

Converting the Abrams kit to 'TUSK' standard was accomplished with the Legend TUSK upgrade and the Voyager rear slat sets. The Legend set is very well engineered and thought out and the Voyager set is also of the highest quality, and for extra realism the set uses a heavier gauge of brass

Besides some Internet hunting, most of the references used for the project were from these two publications. Tankograd's book gives you a nice background on the real TUSK conversion, whilst the elderly 'In-Action' book from Squadron brings some handy generic Abrams details

Lower hull construction commences. The hull side walls were slightly warped inward, so styrene tube was glued in to 'true-up' the sides. Although this may be seen as overkill, I didn't want any alignment problems later when attaching the heavy resin and etch clad skirts

Starting the build, I couldn't resist a quick dry fit to see almost of the major parts fit together. A little warping was evident on the lower hull, but overall no major fit problems were encountered

instances when small detail painting is needed, but for the most part I go by this motto 'if in doubt – take the airbrush out!' On many occasions the extra time spent masking up parts to spray will pay dividends on your finished model. Having clean hands is a must as well! Wash them before handling parts and pieces, and even invest in a set of white cotton gloves to handle the finished model.

Weathering techniques and methods vary from modeller to modeller. The effect I was after was a dry, dusty vehicle that had recently travelled over a hard road surface. After the dark pre-shade coat it was easy to build up highlights and shadows without the finished product looking like a patchwork quilt you see with some pre-shade jobs. As I'm not a fan of dry-brushing large areas or long corners or edges of AFV models I have not employed this technique here, moreover I have let the painting process bring out the details. It is my hope you will gain inspiration to tackle your own Abrams project!

Cleaning all the road wheels is no fun, but this handy gift from my wife made short work of them! A rotary tool clamped in a vice can yield similar results

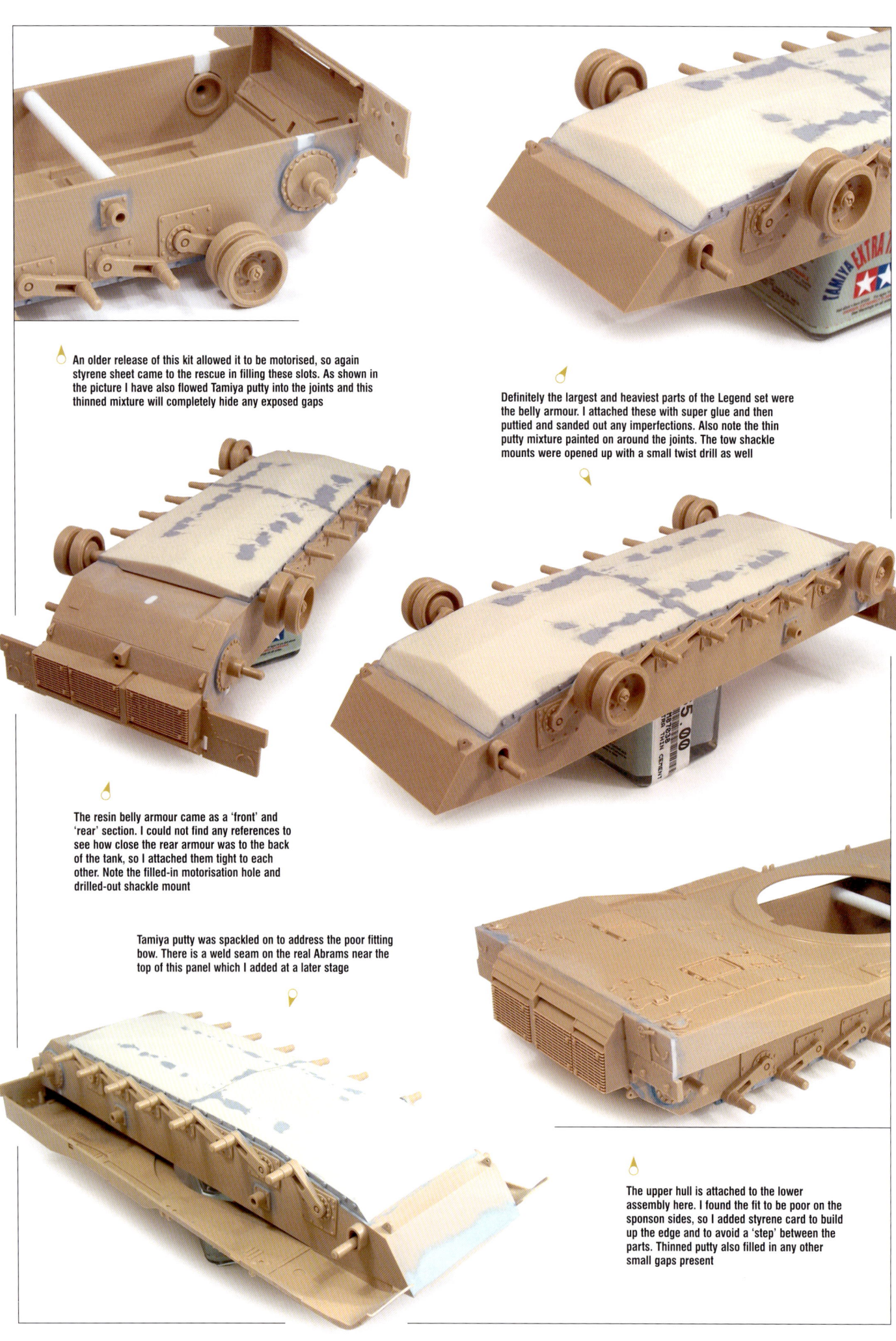

An older release of this kit allowed it to be motorised, so again styrene sheet came to the rescue in filling these slots. As shown in the picture I have also flowed Tamiya putty into the joints and this thinned mixture will completely hide any exposed gaps

Definitely the largest and heaviest parts of the Legend set were the belly armour. I attached these with super glue and then puttied and sanded out any imperfections. Also note the thin putty mixture painted on around the joints. The tow shackle mounts were opened up with a small twist drill as well

The resin belly armour came as a 'front' and 'rear' section. I could not find any references to see how close the rear armour was to the back of the tank, so I attached them tight to each other. Note the filled-in motorisation hole and drilled-out shackle mount

Tamiya putty was spackled on to address the poor fitting bow. There is a weld seam on the real Abrams near the top of this panel which I added at a later stage

The upper hull is attached to the lower assembly here. I found the fit to be poor on the sponson sides, so I added styrene card to build up the edge and to avoid a 'step' between the parts. Thinned putty also filled in any other small gaps present

The non-skid texture was simulated with 'Rustoleum' fine texture paint. This sandy finish leaves the aerosol can nozzle with hurricane force, so masking everything is very important. Now, with the masks removed, I was relieved to see I had the non-skid only where I wanted it!

One of the complaints of the Tamiya Abrams kits is the lack of non-skid surface detail. So using a diagram of the non-skid pattern I laid the outline onto the lower hull deck. Liquid mask was used to completely cover any leftover voids between the masking tape. No shortcuts in this step – it took forever!

Legend advise you to cut away a portion of the kit skirts and replace this with the etch parts included in the upgrade set. This fitted perfectly.

Let's take a moment to discuss attaching etched parts. Most of the brass used in this build was attached using these tools shown. Small etched parts typically were 'tacked' into place with 'Elmer's' glue first. Once the 'Elmer's' was dry, thin superglue was flowed into the area. By using Elmer's first you will have time to adjust the part before applying the permanent fix. Micro brushes by far are the best way to flow the thin super glue onto parts and surfaces

Looking ahead to the skirt assembly, I decided to add styrene rod outriggers to make the attachments easier. Once the locations were measured out on the hull these were glued into place. Note that getting the correct length of these supports was critical; they shouldn't be longer than the sides of the sponson overhang, or the skirts won't be ninety-degrees to the bottom

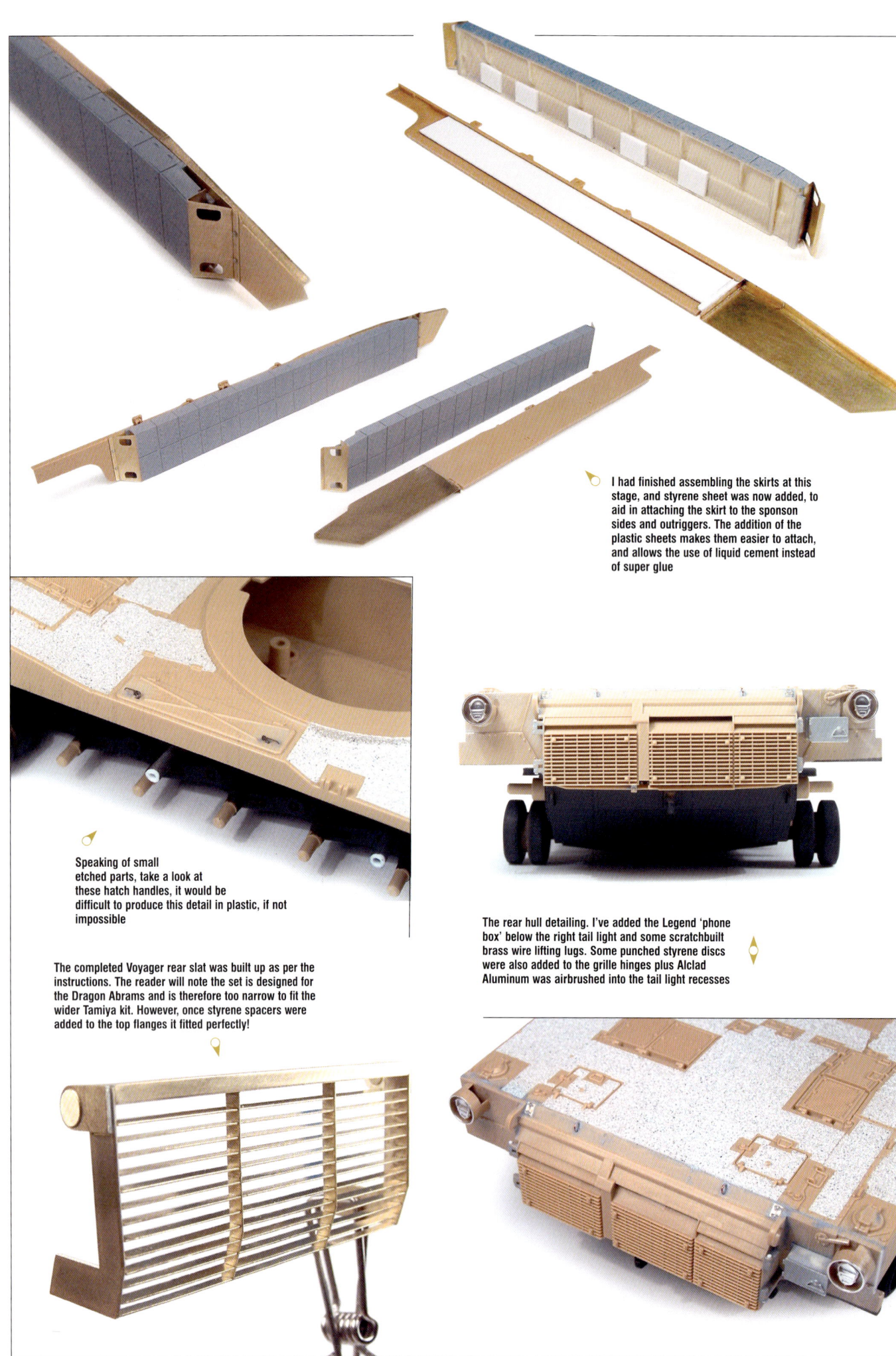

I had finished assembling the skirts at this stage, and styrene sheet was now added, to aid in attaching the skirt to the sponson sides and outriggers. The addition of the plastic sheets makes them easier to attach, and allows the use of liquid cement instead of super glue

Speaking of small etched parts, take a look at these hatch handles, it would be difficult to produce this detail in plastic, if not impossible

The completed Voyager rear slat was built up as per the instructions. The reader will note the set is designed for the Dragon Abrams and is therefore too narrow to fit the wider Tamiya kit. However, once styrene spacers were added to the top flanges it fitted perfectly!

The rear hull detailing. I've added the Legend 'phone box' below the right tail light and some scratchbuilt brass wire lifting lugs. Some punched styrene discs were also added to the grille hinges plus Alclad Aluminum was airbrushed into the tail light recesses

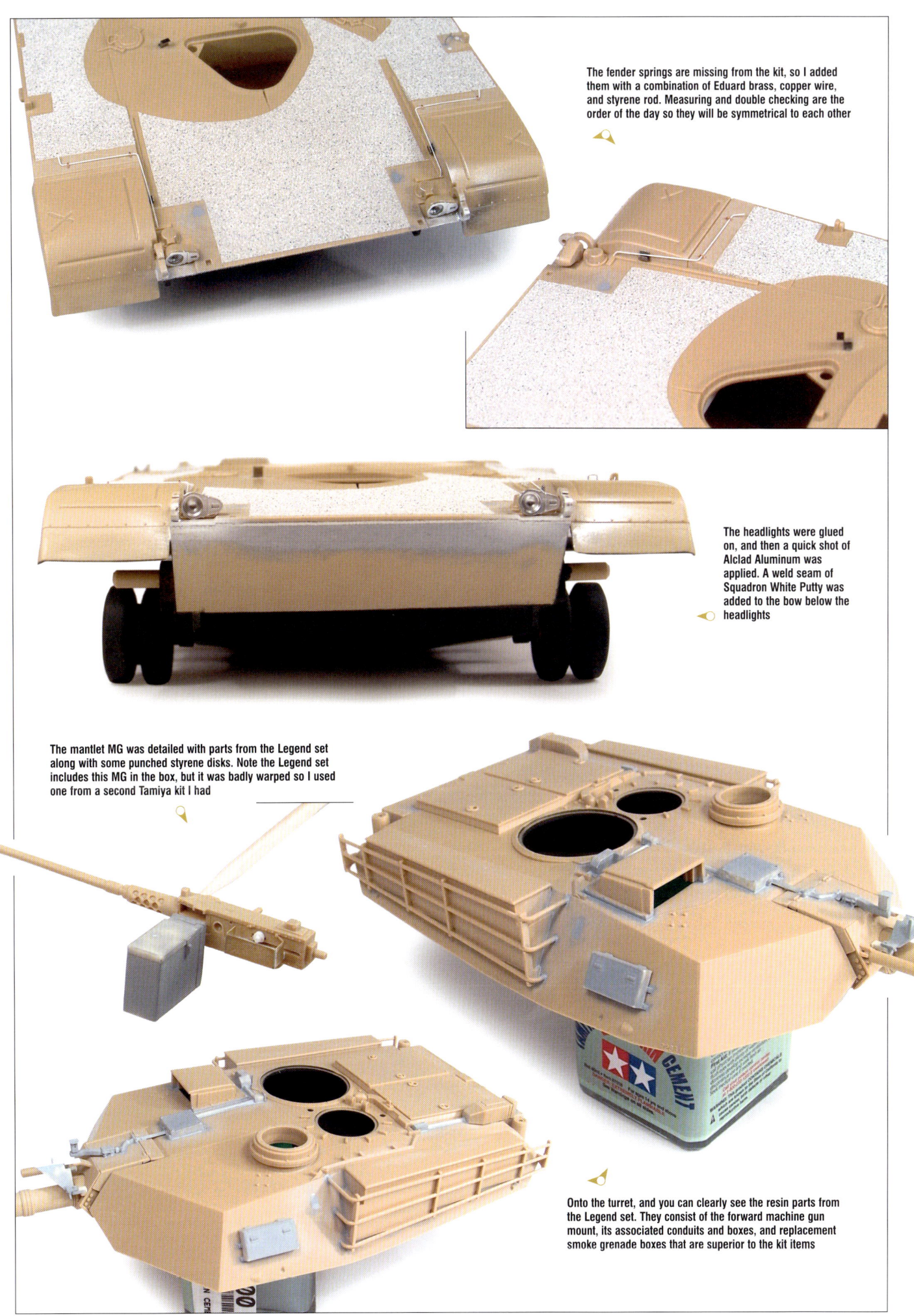

The fender springs are missing from the kit, so I added them with a combination of Eduard brass, copper wire, and styrene rod. Measuring and double checking are the order of the day so they will be symmetrical to each other

The headlights were glued on, and then a quick shot of Alclad Aluminum was applied. A weld seam of Squadron White Putty was added to the bow below the headlights

The mantlet MG was detailed with parts from the Legend set along with some punched styrene disks. Note the Legend set includes this MG in the box, but it was badly warped so I used one from a second Tamiya kit I had

Onto the turret, and you can clearly see the resin parts from the Legend set. They consist of the forward machine gun mount, its associated conduits and boxes, and replacement smoke grenade boxes that are superior to the kit items

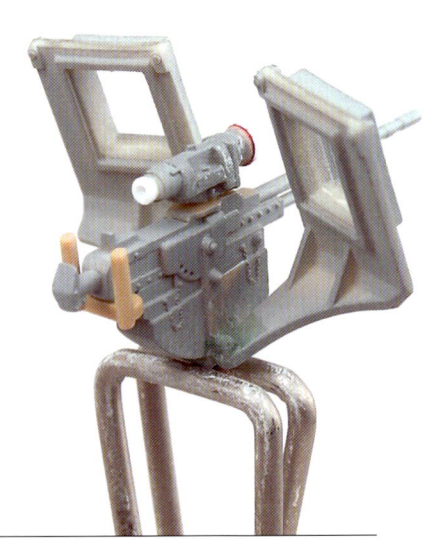

Here the added scratch built details are obvious in this close-up of the loader's MG and gun shield. Again Legend included the gun in the set, but I decided the Tamiya one was easier to work with. Note the barrel has been drilled out and the angle of the gun shields. They are set based on pictures in the Tankograd book, as the Legend box top shows them as straight across, which is incorrect

A clear view to the APU and rear basket, the latter with added Eduard etched mesh

More turret details added, amongst which is the non-skid surface, the Eduard smoke discharger mounts and the Legend loader's supplemental shield. The tow cable was replaced by nylon string and the etched retainers have been added to each side

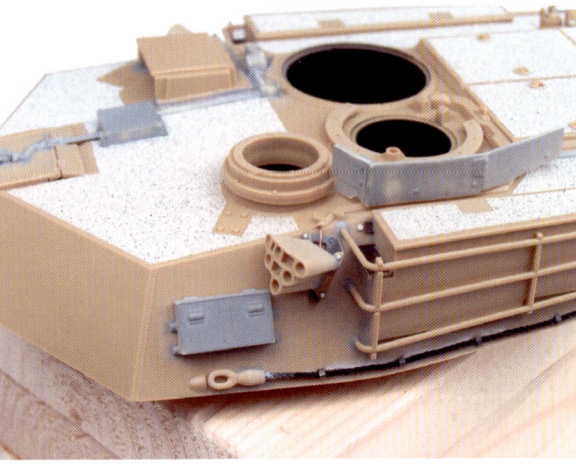

On the lower turret I found myself replacing weld seams. Two strips of Tamiya tape were laid down the width of the seam, and then putty was spread onto the exposed plastic. A chiseled tooth pick is then used to impart weld beads onto the putty. Lastly the tape is pulled up leaving the fresh weld seam

The turret completed. Note the added weld seams below the mantlet and the commander's range finder and CITV viewer. The barrel is from the kit and Tamiya has also thoughtfully designed the commander's cupola as well as other items so they require the clear parts to be added or inserted after painting

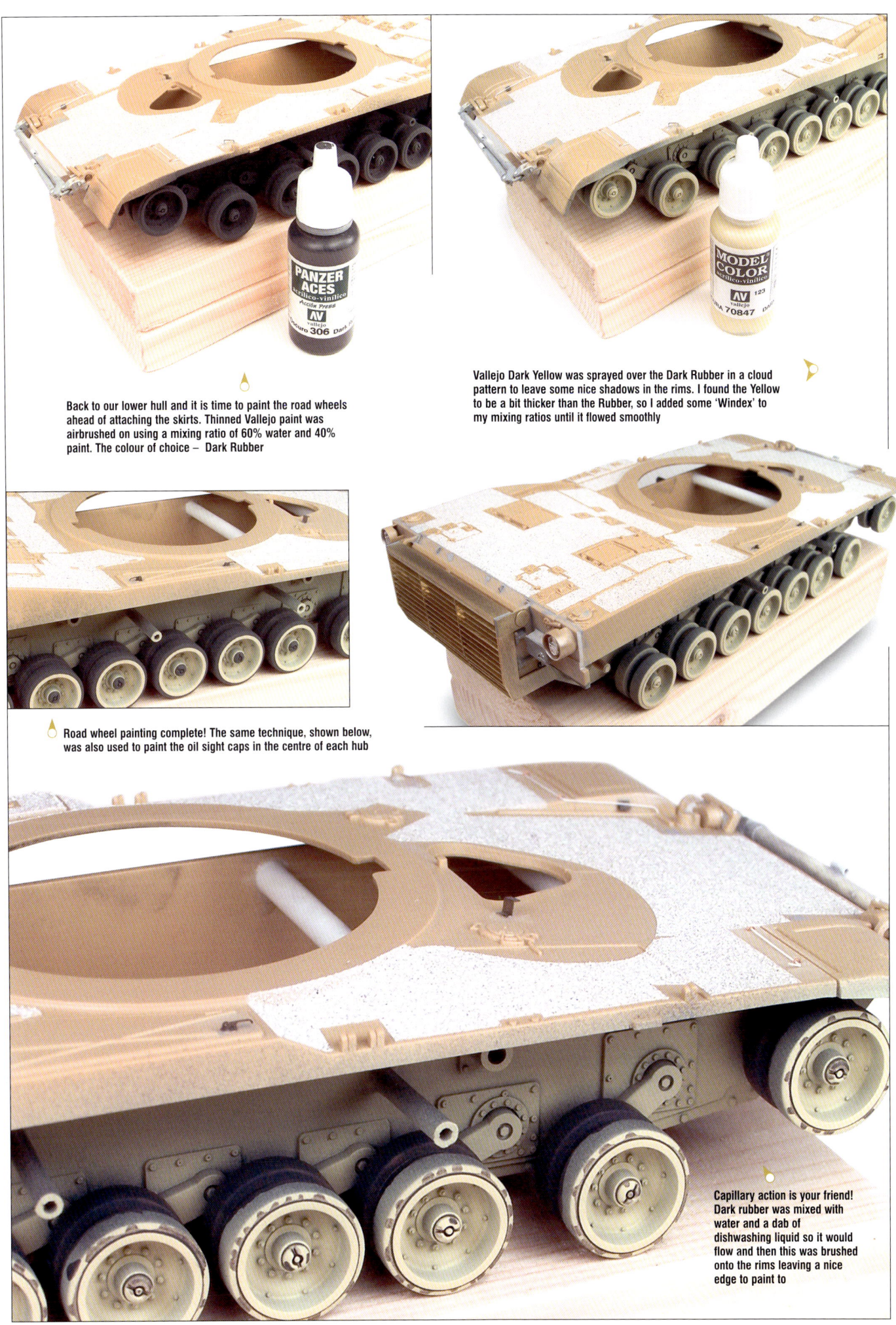

Back to our lower hull and it is time to paint the road wheels ahead of attaching the skirts. Thinned Vallejo paint was airbrushed on using a mixing ratio of 60% water and 40% paint. The colour of choice – Dark Rubber

Vallejo Dark Yellow was sprayed over the Dark Rubber in a cloud pattern to leave some nice shadows in the rims. I found the Yellow to be a bit thicker than the Rubber, so I added some 'Windex' to my mixing ratios until it flowed smoothly

Road wheel painting complete! The same technique, shown below, was also used to paint the oil sight caps in the centre of each hub

Capillary action is your friend! Dark rubber was mixed with water and a dab of dishwashing liquid so it would flow and then this was brushed onto the rims leaving a nice edge to paint to

The skirts are now added after applying non-skid to the tops of each block. All of the measuring and double checking had paid off – they were pretty straight and ninety-degrees to the bottom! Finally etched bolt strips were added to complete the look

The finished model ready for paint!

To avoid fracturing the headlight glass, heat an X-acto knife and slice off the part. It's easy to file off the remaining burnt sprue nib rather than risk frosting or cracking the part under pressure

The lower skirts were masked of then a smooth finish of 'Rustoleum Dark Grey' primer was applied from a can. Heating the can in a tub of hot water really allowed it to flow

The 'Sand' camouflage colour was applied in a cloud pattern letting the pre-shaded dark grey primer show through the panel lines and grille work

Detail painting on the turret using Testors Rubber for the tow cable and Vallejo Dark Rubber for the antennae mounts

After a blast of Future polish, the model was washed with raw umber oil paints. The painted ammunition boxes and extra side bin are from the Legend M1 Stowage set

ODORLESS
turpenoid
turpentine substitute

An odorless thinner for artists' oil colors, oils, and varnishes. Cleans oil painting brushes accessories.

Most shots of TUSK Abrams had unit markings painted out

Tamiya Smoke provided the heat stained centre rear grille as seen in my reference photos

The washed model was then coated with Krylon Matte spray and was now ready for its final weathering

I applied brown Vallejo pigments to the rear grilles and clipped on the rear slat which I had pre-painted in a dark grey colour

The tail lights were added after a quick spray of Tamiya Clear Red

Brown Vallejo pigments were applied dry to the running gear and fixed in place with Turpenoid odorless thinners

Tamiya advise you to you paint the vision blocks after cutting them out of plastic sheet, however I used a plastic folder that was the perfect colour. For the loader's armoured glass I used an aqua coloured CD case

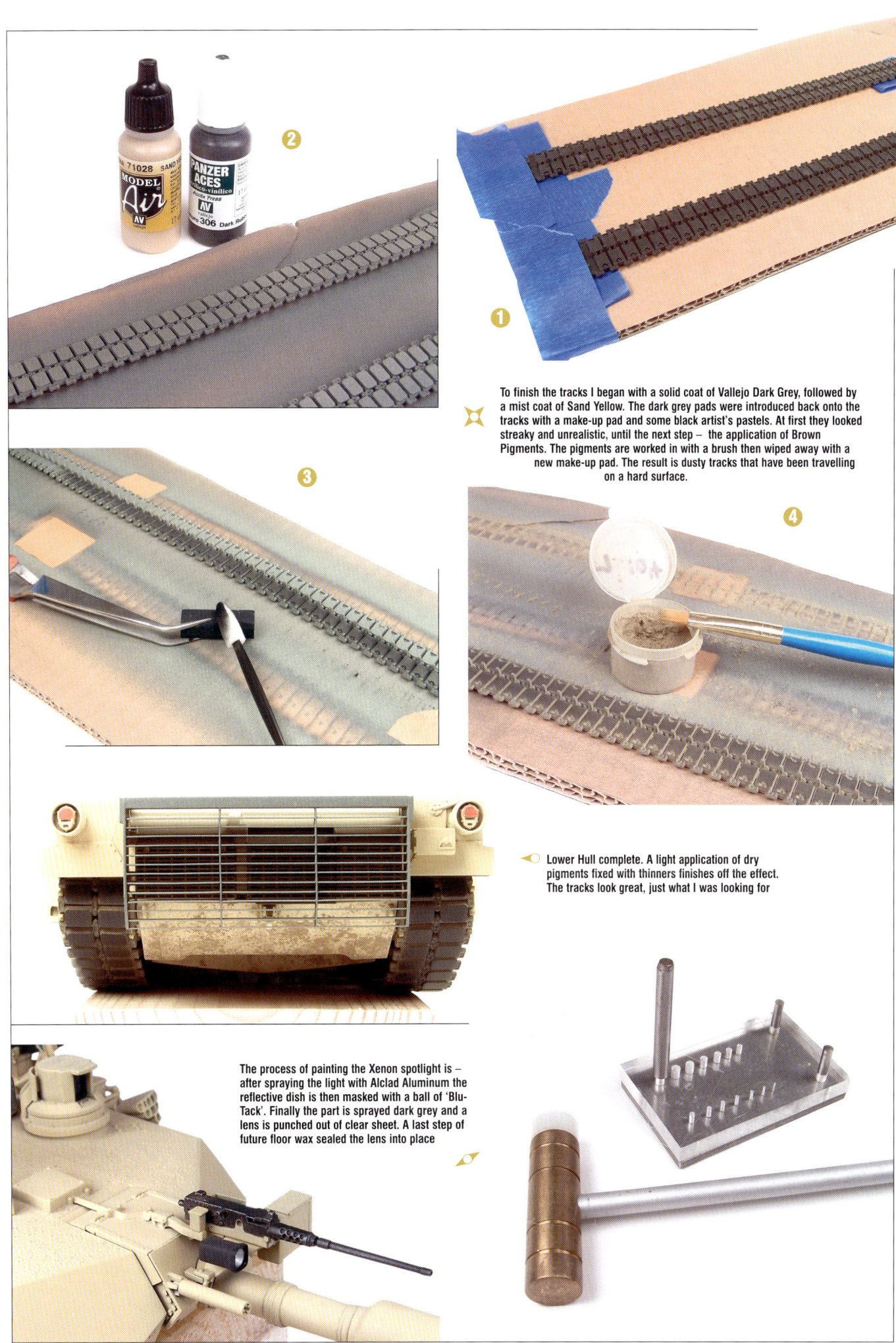

To finish the tracks I began with a solid coat of Vallejo Dark Grey, followed by a mist coat of Sand Yellow. The dark grey pads were introduced back onto the tracks with a make-up pad and some black artist's pastels. At first they looked streaky and unrealistic, until the next step – the application of Brown Pigments. The pigments are worked in with a brush then wiped away with a new make-up pad. The result is dusty tracks that have been travelling on a hard surface.

Lower Hull complete. A light application of dry pigments fixed with thinners finishes off the effect. The tracks look great, just what I was looking for

The process of painting the Xenon spotlight is – after spraying the light with Alclad Aluminum the reflective dish is then masked with a ball of 'Blu-Tack'. Finally the part is sprayed dark grey and a lens is punched out of clear sheet. A last step of future floor wax sealed the lens into place

As mentioned before, the kit allowed the Range Finder and Thermal Viewers glazing to be added from the bottom of the turret, after a coat of black behind the face of the 'glass'. Spraying them from the back allowed the face to be nice and shiny!

The finished model. Tusk upgrades visible are the appliqué Reactive Armour Tiles, the loader's Armoured Gun Shield, and the Counter Sniper 50. Cal mounted to the mantlet

Shown attached to the finished and weathered turret, the loader's machine gun is a real focal point of the model. The attachment of the 'glass' was the same as for the spotlight, with Future firmly cementing the panels in place

The commander's 50 cal. is basically the Tamiya part with the Legend ammunition box suitably painted

Rear RPG protection is another TUSK upgrade

The V-shaped under-armour is well visible in this shot. This boat hull shaped armour affords additional protection for IED's detonated under the tank

A close-up of the extra detailing done to the front fenders. An application of sand coloured pigments was brushed onto the surface then wiped away leaving it in the low spots, dark corners and recesses

I thought it a nice touch to paint the large stowage box a lighter shade of sand to simulate a field modified add-on

2

Bradley Infantry Fighting Vehicle (IFV)

The introduction of the tank into the battlefields during World War I brought with it a new problem for the military. Though tanks possessed superior armour and firepower and could roll into enemy territory with virtual immunity, it was quickly discovered that without infantry support any gains by the armoured presence could be quickly lost. Infantry had to be able to keep up with the armour, not only to secure lines pushed forward by the tanks, but also to protect them from other hostile forces. Oddly enough, this caused the tank to be regulated to infantry support!

As the 20th century progressed, the US Army was keen on this issue, and used the M2 and M3 halftracks to bring infantry forward to the front with the armour. However, their weakness of open tops and thin armour became very apparent and standard practice was to ride near the lines, then the infantry would disembark to engage the enemy. The Army realised that the infantry truly needed an armoured carrier to take them to the front line. This led to a series of experiments and adaptations to try to come up with an Armoured Personnel Carrier. This eventually led to the first widespread and very successful design of the M113 which is still used today. With a successful APC for the infantry, it did not take long for the soldiers to begin to use it in a more aggressive role with mounted machine guns, recoilless rifles, and armoured shields. There was even one variant, the XM734, that had firing ports along the side for infantry to shoot from inside the vehicle. Though usable in this role, a true ground-up design for an Infantry Fighting Vehicle (IFV) was needed.

The first design was the XM701 MICV-65 (Mechanized Infantry Combat Vehicle-1965). With its enclosed turret, firing ports, front mounted engine, and rear troop compartment we begin to see the familiar lines of the Bradley M2 series. The MICV-65 was too slow and heavy, plus the cost of the war in Vietnam forced the Army to cancel the project. At the same time,

This M2A2 in April of 2003 rolls near a presidential palace in Bagdad. It displays several "early" features such as the thin turret hatch, lack of armour on the rear overhead hatch, and smooth barrel. Note the CIP (Combat Identification Panel) panels and ample gear *(© US Army)*

This Bradley of Task Force 64, 3rd ID early in the war is covered in stowed gear within side stowage racks. Note the many 20mm ammo cans on the turret for additional stowage space. Early ODS features include a non-fluted barrel, old style frontal armour, and revised sight housing, or 'dog house' *(© John Moore)*

A M2A2 during early 2004. This Bradley shows a few of the ODS features, such as the revised sight housing and exhaust. The Tamiya kit out of the box will give the modeler this version. Note the large amount of stowed gear, common early in the war *(© unknown via J Nelson)*

FMC submitted a design of a heavily modified M-113 that became the XM-765, and though not adopted by the US Army, it was sold to other countries as the YPR-765. This vehicle shows even more characteristics of the future Bradley design. During the mid 1970's the US Army had two programs – one aimed at replacing the M-551 and M114 in the Cavalry scout role, and the other being the MICV project. Realising the current political atmosphere was not going to fund two projects, the Army merged the two and issued new requirements. FMC had already been developing an improved version of their XM-765 design, the XM723, and used that as a basis to begin work meeting the new requirements for both an Infantry Fighting Vehicle (XM-2), and Cavalry Fighting Vehicle (XM-3).

This Bradley is interesting in that the crew has attached several 20mm ammo cans along the skirts. The revised exhaust can be seen a bit more clearly here, and the crew has added some sandbags for additional protection, or maybe ready for use to build a hasty infantry fighting position. An Iraqi BMP burns in the background *(© John Moore)*

A M2A2 helps crush a Saddam monument in the city of Al Hawijah late 2003. From the lack of stowed gear, this vehicle is most likely out on a daily patrol and appears to have driven through some thick mud and sludge that caused the crew to remove the rearmost skirt, which sits atop the side armour. Also no TOW missiles are loaded. We also see a number of the ODS features, including a fluted barrel, armour panels on the rear overhead hatch, and thicker turret hatch *(© US Army)*

This picture of a Bradley undergoing an engine change out gives us an excellent view of the power-pack. Being in a hostile environment, the mechanics all wear their Kevlar helmets. They also wear one-piece Nomex suits that are issued to all armoured vehicle crewmen (© US Army)

Another view of the power-pack, a Cummins VTA-903T diesel. With 600 horsepower, the Bradley can travel up to 45mph on land, and is able to keep up with the Abrams (© US Army, Sgt David Turner)

Not the view to see during a vehicle inspection, but with the power-pack hoisted by the M88, we can see down into the engine compartment. Working order in a combat environment is far more important than cleanliness (© US Army, Sgt Jeremi Timb)

Late in 2004, ERA blocks began to be installed on Bradleys as standard kit. This M2A2 Bradley Fighting Vehicle from 1st Platoon, Alpha Troop, 1-4 Cavalry, 1st Infantry Division moves into an over watch position at a traffic control point outside of Ad Duluyiah, Iraq. Under the coat of dust, it appears that this Bradley was originally painted in the three-tone NATO scheme of brown, black, and green (© US Army)

A pair of M6 Linebacker vehicles from the 7th Cavalry. They are on patrol along a stretch of roadway that was renowned for insurgents planting IED bombs along the road. The Linebacker was already slated to be retired, and is now no longer in service *(© US Army)*

This Bradley, a M2A2, patrols a street following a grenade attack by insurgents. The crew has removed almost all of the side skirting, and the one remaining CIP panel on the rear shows signs of an impact, maybe from backing into a object, or another vehicle hitting this Bradley. The vehicle commander carries a M4 at the ready. The hatches, as seen in most pictures, are always open and rarely have I seen pictures of the doors shut *(© US Army)*

A soldier from the 1st ID looks over his favourite magazine in the back of a M2A2. 'Pepsi' appears to be the drink of choice, or at least what is available. Note the older style ALICE pack and Day-Glo IFF panel on the top of the vehicle. Of interest are the various colours the vision periscopes take depending on how the light hits them. This is due to the anti-laser layer to prevent eye damage from targeting lasers *(© US Army)*

Looking up at the turret of a passing M2A2, we get a good view of the coaxial M240G machine gun, as well as the ballistic glass cupola around the commander's hatch. This allows him to have his head outside the hatch, yet protects against IED shrapnel and snipers. Also note how the 25mm is elevated, but the mantlet remains level with the turret. Both the Tamiya and Academy kits have this wrong and elevate the entire front of the turret with the gun *(© US Army)*

This Bradley is interesting as the crew has added several hand holds along the front armour plate to help aid the driver entering and exiting the vehicle. Even though this Bradley sports some armoured glass around the commander's station, it still shows many early ODS features, such as the early nose armour and the crew platform along the left side of the turret. Note that the smoke grenade stowage boxes on either side of the main gun are green, and not tan *(© US Army)*

Bradleys from the 3rd Infantry Division, Task Force Liberty, at an Iraqi police traffic control check point in Tikrit, Iraq. On this M2A2, we see the newer style front nose armour. Compare to previous pictures and there are slight differences. Also note that the left smoke grenade stowage box has been relocated above the other *(© US Army)*

First, the one man turret was replaced with a two-man turret, mounting a 25mm 'Bushmaster' cannon, plus a TOW missile launcher to give the vehicle the ability to deal with the latest Soviet tanks. In the XM-2, provision was made for a full squad of seven in the rear with each having a firing port through the sides or rear ramp. The XM-2 carried only two in the rear, however filled the rest of the space with extra ammunition and TOW rounds for longer sustained 'Calvary Scout' missions. The Army accepted the designs as the M2 and M3, naming it after General Omar Bradley, with final approval for production coming from the Secretary of Defence on 1 February 1980. Since entering active service in 1981, a total of 6,724 Bradleys (4,641 M2s and 2,083 M3s) have been produced. Hard to imagine that thirty years after its initial acceptance, it still serves on the front line.

The M2 IFV and M3 CIV Bradley

The overall mission of the M2/M3 series can be summed up in three points:

- Safely transport infantry to critical locations on the battlefield
- Provide fire support to cover their dismounted operations
- Destroy enemy tanks and other vehicles that may threaten the infantry it carries

The infantry version (M2) is used most often to close with the enemy by means of fire and manoeuvre. The primary tasks performed by the cavalry version (M3) as part of a troop and/or squadron is reconnaissance, security and flank guard missions. Even with these differing missions, the overall appearance of the two vehicles is almost identical, and both share most major components. The most distinguishing external difference between the M2 and M3 is that the M3 has all of the firing ports removed and plated over and the rearmost periscopes along the rear of the troop compartment are located in the overhead hatch on the M3.

The hull of the Bradley series is constructed of welded aluminium and spaced laminate armour. In addition, the M2A2/M3A2 Bradleys have appliqué steel armour plates along the sides with provision for additional passive armour or explosive reactive armour (ERA). The ERA consists of ninety-six tiles fixed to the sides, turret and front of the vehicle, which enhance protection against a variety of anti-armour munitions including shoulder-launched Rocket Propelled Grenades (RPG). With the IED threat found in Iraq, BAe Systems installed Improvised Explosive Device (IED) mine armour on 433 Bradley M2/M3 vehicles.

For the powerplant, the Bradley originally used the 500hp Cummins VTA 903 T turbo charged diesel with the HMPT-500 Hydromechanical transmission. That has now been upgraded with the M2A2 to a 600hp engine. This gives the Bradley a top speed of around 45mph on a hard surface and a range of 300 miles. This allows it to keep pace with the M1 Abrams, which was developed and fielded in about the same timeframe as the IFV project, allowing the infantry it carries to be available as the armoured force moves forward and engages the enemy.

Armament

The M2/M3's main armament is a McDonnell Douglas M242 25mm 'Bushmaster' cannon capable of firing up to 200 rounds per minute and is accurate up to 2,500m depending on the ammunition used. The M242 has an integrated dual-feed mechanism and remote ammunition selection. Either armour piercing (APDS-T) or high explosive (HE) ammunition may be selected with the flick of a switch. The gunner may select from single or multiple shot modes. It is also armed with twin TOW-2B missiles which are capable of destroying most tanks out to a maximum range of 3,750m. However, the TOW missiles can only

A 4th Cavalry Bradley leaves Forward Operating Base MacKenzie in Iraq for a mission on Oct. 30, 2004. Another nice example of tan ERA blocks on a green painted Bradley. The driver appears to be wearing the inside liner of the CVC helmet without the Kevlar shell
(© Shane A Cuomo, US Air Force)

One of the Bradley variants to see limited use was the M6 Linebacker. This version has a four-tube Stinger missile launcher and additional sighting equipment to make a dedicated air-defense vehicle. They retain the 25mm Bushmaster cannon. This vehicle is from the 7th Cavalry
(© US Army)

Another M2A2 of the 3rd ID manning a three-way stop. The tow cable has been stowed in such a way to provide quick usage in the case of a breakdown. Each vehicle caries one, and between two vehicles they have the two cables needed to make a recovery. The complete lack of external gear shows this crew to be not far from home base, but also external gear is a fire hazard if hit with a RPG or IED *(© US Army, Spc Mary Rose)*

Another green M2A2 seen at a range near Mada'in Qad, Iraq. This one is interesting in that you see the large, 3-band overhead wire deflector on the turret roof. This not only keeps the vehicle from being caught in low hanging overhead wires, but also protects the crew from any taught wires stretched for malicious intent *(© US Army, Pfc Michael Schuch)*

Prime example of the protection afforded by the ballistic glass. This is the result of the shrapnel from a 155mm based IED that went off near a vehicle. These kits are also found on the Stryker, Abrams, Hummer, and even fitted on USMC AAVP-7 vehicles *(© US Army)*

An up-close and personal look at the business end of the 25mm M242 Bushmaster cannon. The vehicle carries 300 rounds ready and another 600 stowed in the M2, and 1,200 stowed in the M3. The ready rounds are divided between two boxes, which can be loaded with two different types of ammunition, selected on demand depending on what is needed. Both armour piercing M791 APDS-T rounds and M792 HEI-T, high explosive incendiary are available

It's not too often that we get pictures of both sides of the same vehicle and taken within minutes of each other. This M2A2 of the 130th Infantry regiment, Illinois Army National Guard, shows a mix of early and late ODS features. It still retains the crew platform, but does have the updated nose armour, thickened turret hatch, fluted barrel, and other features along with the ERA blocks *(© US Army)*

The right side of the same Army National Guard M2A2. Note that the colour of the hull itself is a very light green. There are pictures of Abrams tanks painted in this same green. The scale model built in this book uses these photos as a basis *(© US Army)*

Instant roadblock and checkpoint! A M2A2 stares down civilian vehicles making their way along a road. The Bradley appears to be painted in the three-tone European scheme and has early features, such as the style of armour on the nose. There is a unusual bracket on the front plate *(© US Army)*

A very interesting shot showing an M2A2 undergoing maintenance at Camp Ramadi, Iraq. With all the side skirts removed, we get a good view of the running gear plus the mounting strips for the External Reactive Armour (ERA). Of interest is the mix of early and later type ammo can brackets along the turret stowage basket. The one on the far left is a earlier type with the two footman loops *(© US Army)*

be fired while the vehicle is stationary. Several types of TOW missiles have been developed, including anti-armour and bunker busting types. The Bradley also carries an M240C coaxial 7.62 mm medium machine gun, located to the right of the 25 mm chain gun. The Bradley is also equipped with two M257 smoke grenade dischargers, each loaded with four smoke grenades, and is fitted with an engine smoke-generating system.

Variants

Among improvements on the basic M2 and M3 design, the series has been widely modified. Its chassis is the basis for the M270 Multiple Launch Rocket System, the M4 C2V Battlefield Command Post, and the M6 Bradley 'Linebacker' Air Defense Vehicle. Its suspension system has also been used on versions of

the US Marines AAV with the RAM/RS upgrade program. Here is a basic description of each ICV/IFV Bradley variant to see service so far:

M2/M3

The M2 (also sometimes written M2A0 to help prevent confusion) was the basic production model, first produced in 1982. The M2A0 can be identified by its standard TOW missile system and 500 horsepower (370 kW) engine with HMPT-500 Hydromechanical transmission. Basic features also included an integrated sight unit for the M242 25mm, and thermal imaging system. For the IFV, there was seating for up to seven infantrymen in the rear of the vehicle, with the CFV holding a total of two and using the extra room to store additional

Soldiers from Delta Company, 1st Battalion, 8th Infantry Regiment, load up inside their Bradley M2A2 Infantry Fighting Vehicle after conducting a cordon and search operation at Al Intisar, Mosul, Iraq. Of note is that this Bradley has the Rhino ECM anti-IED antenna installed on the left tail light cover. Notice the chipping, dents, and weathering of the ERA blocks. A camouflage net has been erected over the wire deflectors on the turret to add some concealment against snipers while the crew is exposed in the open hatches *(© US Army)*

Another great picture of an M2A2 with the ERA blocks removed. Note the different style of brackets used on the turret, front, and hull sides. This vehicle is also an earlier ODS as it has the early nose armour plate, but does have the fluted barrel, new exhaust, and other minor modifications. The large number of in-theatre Bradleys show the large variation of colours, markings, and features present on these vehicles *(© US Army)*

ammunition for the 25mm and TOW launcher. The M2A0 was amphibious with the use of a 'Swim Barrier' or 'Floatation Screen'. It was C-141 and C-5 transportable, meeting the requirements by the Army to be air-transportable. All M2A0 vehicles have been upgraded to improved standards.

M2A1/M3A1

Introduced in 1986, the A1 variant included an improved TOW-2 missile system, a Gas Particulate Filter Units (GPFU) NBC system, and a fire-suppression system. The TOW-2 rockets had a larger warhead, improved fuel, and faster. With these improvements, the TOW was able to deal with the new generation Russian tanks such as the T-64 and T-72. Other improvements and changes included a redesigned turret stowage rack, improved floatation screens, and some other minor improvements. By 1992, the M2A1s had begun being remanufactured to upgraded standards.

M2A2/ M3A2

As intelligence discovered newer advances in Soviet weapons, it became aware that the Bradley's composite armour would not be sufficient. With the A2 upgrade program, the composite armour skirts were replaced by a steel armour plate, 1-1/4 inch thick, on the sides and front of the vehicle. On the plates provisions was made to mount ERA blocks. With the additional weight, the engine was upgraded to 600hp to keep performance from being hindered. Other changes included stronger torsion bars, deleted trim vane, and spall liners in the troop compartment. Also the seating was adjusted to a bench style in order to make dismounting easier, plus the additional armour plating on the sides of the vehicle had made firing-port weapons irrelevant. Production began in 1988, and most A1's were upgraded to the A2 standard.

M2A3 / M3A3

The US Army A3 Bradley upgrade program includes improvements based on operational experience in the Gulf War. The first low-rate initial production M2A3/M3A3 Bradley was delivered in November 1998 and entered service in April 2000. The system was approved for full-rate production in May 2001. Over 620 vehicles have so far been upgraded. The upgrade of a further 120 vehicles was ordered in February 2005. In June 2005, a contract for the upgrade of an additional 450 vehicles to A3 standard was placed. In August 2006, a follow-on contract was awarded for 96 vehicles, and in November 2006, for an additional 610. In July 2007 a further 172 vehicles were

This shot provides a nice close-up of the front corner of the Bradley turret. The crew has the wire deflectors attached, and note how they bolt to the lift rings. Also there is a wire mesh over the sight glass to protect it from thrown objects. The stencil text on the sight doors reads **'CAUTION DO NOT PUSH/PULL DOOR USE INTERNAL HANDLE ONLY'** *(© US Army)*

The M2A3 and M3A3 were introduced later in the Iraq conflict. The most noticeable change is the addition of the Commander's Independent Viewer (CIV), at the right rear of the turret. This includes a FLIR and an electro-optical/TV imaging system, among other targeting and range finding improvements. The CIV allows the commander to scan for targets and maintain situational awareness while remaining under armour. This M2A3 is at Camp Rustamiyah, IQ and crewed by soldiers from 1st Battalion, 8th Cavalry Regiment, 2nd Infantry Brigade Combat Team (IBCT), 2nd ID attached to 1st Cavalry Division *(© US Army)*

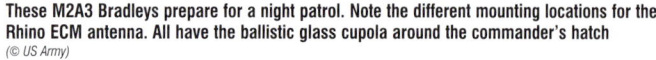

These M2A3 Bradleys prepare for a night patrol. Note the different mounting locations for the Rhino ECM antenna. All have the ballistic glass cupola around the commander's hatch *(© US Army)*

This Bradley fighting vehicle near Muqdadiyah, Iraq shows an interesting mix of external gear and some dark green ERA panels on the front. Traffic cones are stowed as is a box of MREs. The object tied to the left armour skirt is a fire blanket container *(© US Army)*

Using an M3A3, soldiers from Charlie Company, 2nd Battalion – 162nd Infantry (2-162 Infantry) out of Patrol Base Volunteer set up perimeter security. Compare the relative lack of external gear, markings, and damage to this Bradley against those seen earlier in the conflict. Most units operate out of small local bases, and for short periods of time while coordinating and training local Iraqi security personnel. All part of the newer strategy implemented in 2006 to combat insurgents that has since proven quite successful *(© US Army)*

A pair of Bradleys on patrol
(© US Army)

A M2A2 Bradley fighting
vehicle from 1st Battalion,
12th Cavalry Regiment
provides security in the town
of Tahrir, Iraq, July 2007. Only
the middle portions of the
front ERA blocks have been
installed, and even a few of
those are missing. Some of
the blocks are green, as is
the exhaust cover *(© US Army,
Sgt 1st Class Robert C Brogan)*

This M2A2 Bradley fighting vehicle from 2nd BN, 7th CR, 4th BCT, 1st Cavalry Division illustrates clearly some of the challenges of operating armoured vehicles in an urban environment as it transits a road in Mosul, Iraq. Many narrow roads and alleys can only be patrolled on foot, either due to size limitations imposed by the vehicle width, or due to the dangers of being vulnerable to foot attacks in such close quarters
(© US Army, Sgt Amanda Davis)

A U.S. Army M3A3 Bradley fighting vehicle from Troop G, 2nd Squadron, 3rd Armoured Cavalry Regiment finds a great over-watch position on top of this hill near Mansuriyat al Jabal, Iraq. The front ERA blocks are not installed, and there is only one TOW missile loaded. Other than the 'G33' this Bradley shows no other markings or external gear
(© US Army, Staff Sgt Jason Robertson)

Bradleys move through the downtown streets of Muqdadiyah, Iraq as part of a massive Coalition Forces operation involving Iraqi Security Forces and soldiers from the 6-9 Armoured Reconnaissance Squadron, 3rd Brigade Combat Team, **1st Cav** *(© US Army)*

contracted and the US Army's total requirement is for 2,545 upgraded Bradley A3 vehicles. The upgrade includes the improved Bradley Acquisition System (IBAS) from DRS Technologies for the TOW-2 missile and a Raytheon Commander's Independent Thermal Viewer (CITV), which use second generation thermal imagers derived from the US Army's Horizontal Technology Initiative (HTI), with the imagers based on a 480×4 scanning infrared focal plane array. The IBAS also has day TV and direct view optics, automatic dual target tracking, eye-safe laser rangefinder and two-axis stabilized head mirror. The thermal imaging DRS Technologies driver's vision enhancer (DVE), AN\VAS-5, uses a 320×240 uncooled ferroelectric scanning array. A combat identification system is also being installed. The electronics system includes a data bus with central processors and digital information displays for commander, driver and squad leader, bringing the 30 year old design into the digital battlefield of the 21st century.

A Bradley cautiously moves past a burning truck *(© US Army)*

M6 Linebacker

The M6 Bradley Linebacker was developed during the late 1990's as part of a program to provide protection against fast, low flying aircraft, helicopters, and cruise missiles. Consisting of the M2A2(ODS) Bradley with an integrated, externally mounted four-tube FIM-92A Stinger launcher and integrated position, navigation, and north seeker capability, it can engage targets while stationary or on the move. A total of ninety-nine M6 Linebacker units were delivered to the US Army. In February 2005, United Defense (now BAe Systems Land and Armament) was awarded a contract from the US Army's Tank-automotive and Armaments Command as part of the RESET program to remove the Stinger missile systems from eighty-eight Bradley Linebackers and convert the vehicles to standard M2A2 ODS infantry fighting vehicles. With that conversion being done, the unique M6 Linebacker is no longer in front line service, but did serve a brief time in Iraq.

BUSK Program

The 'Bradley Urban Survivability Kit' or 'BUSK' consists of minor improvements to enhance the Bradley's effectiveness in the urban combat environment. This kit includes a high-powered, hand-held directional spotlight, sight protection for the turret external optics consisting of a mesh encased in a steel frame and a lightweight, non-conductive 'dome tent' structure to protect turret and crew from low-hanging electrical power lines. A further update also includes fire detection/suppression systems and advanced survivability seats. A Commander's Light Automatic Weapon (CLAW), and a 5.56mm light machine gun integrated with the A3 fire control system is under development for the BUSK, as well as additional armour to counter the effects of mines and IED's. Syracuse Research Corporation is supplying

Troop G, 2nd Squadron, 3rd Armoured Cavalry Regiment, provides security in support of 'Operation Raider Harvest' in Muqdadiyah, IQ. This Bradley is a M3A3 which can be discerned barely by the overhead hatch-mounted periscopes and lack of firing ports on the rear ramp. A sign warns in English and Arabic to stay away from the vehicle. A security precaution for the crew against suicide bombers on foot and in cars that may attempt to attack the Bradley by detonating explosives near the vehicle *(© US Army)*

The Bradley's 25mm M242 Bushmaster cannon in action! *(© US Army)*

A 'knocked-out' Bradley
(© US Army)

CREW-2 electronic warfare systems for 1691 Bradley vehicles. CREW-2 is designed to jam remotely controlled IEDs to prevent the detonation of roadside bombs.

Combat

Operation Desert Storm was the first taste of combat for the Bradley after almost eight years of service with the Army. By the time ground combat started, the US had committed almost all of its armoured and mechanised units from the US and Europe. Other than some acclimation to the harsh desert climate, and some initial troubles with the M2A2 transmission, the Bradley served very well and continued to be a part of the main driving force. During the conflict, Bradleys are accredited for destroying more Iraqi armoured vehicles than the M1 Abrams. Twenty Bradleys were lost - three to enemy fire and seventeen to

'friendly fire' incidents; another twelve were damaged. It was the alarming number of 'friendly fire' incidences that led to the development of the CIP panel used widely today.

In Operation Iraqi Freedom, the Bradley has proved somewhat vulnerable to mobility kills from IED and RPG attacks which do not necessarily destroy the vehicle completely, but render it inoperable or immobile, such as track or engine malfunctions. Casualties have been light, due to the adequate armour protection, to allow the crew to escape at the expense of the vehicle. As of early 2006, total losses (including non-combat incidents) were at fifty Bradleys. Lessons learned from this experience are now being reflected in the BUSK program and in modified doctrine for the Bradley's use in the urban, asymmetric warfare environment.

A line of Bradelys waiting their call to duty. Note the oil drip pans under the front of each. The second to last vehicle with the red cross is a medical M113 armored personnel carrier' *(© US Army)*

2

Bradley Walkaround

The upgraded Bradley has the IBAS acquisition system for TOW missiles and a commander's independent thermal viewer (CITV). The IBAS also has day TV and direct view optics, automatic dual target tracking, eyesafe laser rangefinder and two-axis stabilised head mirror *(© Joel Russ)*

This image shows what appears to be a hit near the exhaust, possibly just a glancing impact from a RPG as it appears the damage to be mostly superficial. We do see to good effect the new style exhaust shroud and four-point tie-downs on the side armor plate *(© Joel Russ)*

Looking across the sloping frontal section and turret. Note the position of the spare wheel *(© Joel Russ)*

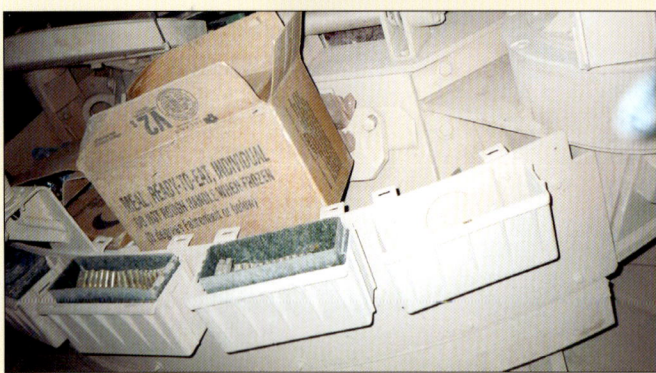

MRE box and shells *(© Joel Russ)*

Looking at the TOW missile 'box' on the turret. Note also the reduced visibility 'stars and bars' *(© Joel Russ)*

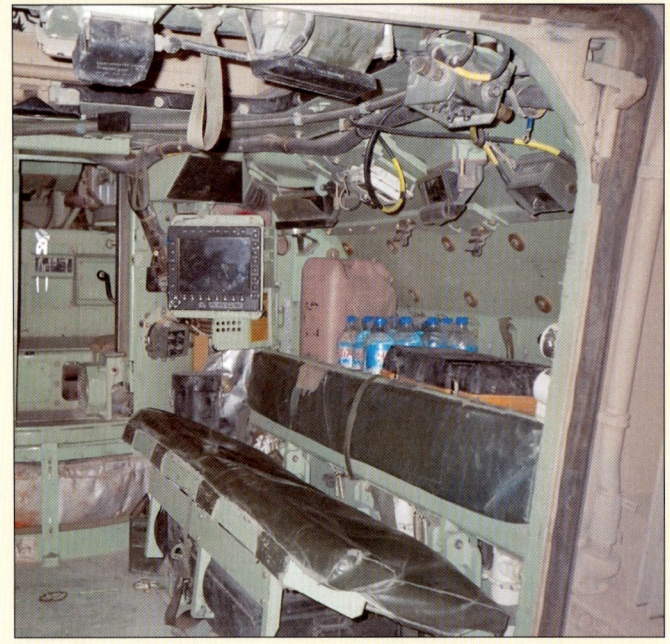

Bradley interior *(© Joel Russ)*

ERA tiles applied to the sides of the vehicle

The Bradley is equipped with two M257 smoke grenade dischargers, each loaded with four smoke grenades *(© Corey Sanders)*

A detail shot of the TOW launcher on an M2A3. The TOW launcher hasn't changed much over the Bradley's lineage, except for improvements to allow the firing of TOW-2 missiles *(© US Army)*

Slots for the ERA tiles *(© Corey Sanders)*

Bradley rear aspect
(© Corey Sanders)

The gunner is equipped with a Raytheon integrated sight unit (ISU) which includes a day / thermal sight with ×4 and ×12 magnification. An optical relay provides the image of the gunner's sight to the commander *(© Joel Russ)*

Soldiers relax while in a rear base. This shot affords a glimpse at the inside, as well as details on the stowed external gear, including the many stowage boxes. Note that the interior seating consists of bench seats. This replaced the old style single-seat system used in the M2A1 and early M2A2 variants

Close-in on the IBAS acquisition system for TOW (Choice) *(© Corey Sanders)*

The main armament is the 25mm M242 Bushmaster chain gun. The M242 has a single barrel with an integrated dual feed mechanism and remote feed selection *(© Corey Sanders)*

The standard Bushmaster rate of fire is 200 rounds a minute but the gun is optionally converted to 500 rounds a minute *(© Corey Sanders)*

Close-in on the fixing point for one of the ERA tiles *(© Corey Sanders)*

Details of the ballistic glass cupola *(© Robert Skipper)*

One of the subtle changes between the A2 and A3 models is the revised sight housing. Note the newer housing is taller, and lacks the upper horizontal cover. With the new sights came increased capability with the fire control software – FCSW, bringing a similar capability to that of the M1A2 Abrams *(© Robert Skipper)*

The CIV turret. Information from the CIV is fed to the Commander's Tactical Display (CTD) and presents information from fire control, targeting, and navigation systems on a moving-map display. This display also shows information about vehicle status and other units that are linked *(© Robert Skipper)*

The rear side of the improved sight housing, or 'doghouse'. The three tubes are for holding range flags while at practice gunnery ranges *(© Robert Skipper)*

Front quarter view of M2A3 with a CIP panel

A heavily laden Bradley, showing stowage positions for equipment

The difference between a M2 and M3 are few externally. From the rear, M2 Bradleys all still have the rear ramp firing ports, plus have the rear facing periscopes mounted on the hull above the rear ramp vs. the M3 which has them mounted inside the overhead hatch *(© US Army)*

Close-in on the IBAS acquisition system for TOW (Choice)

Another shot of the CIV. Note that turret has its head in, down in the secured protected position *(© Robert Skipper)*

2 Bradley Profiles

Bradley IFV M2A2 ODS
1st Battalion, 26th Infantry Regiment, US Army
While the tank wears the original three-tone camouflage pattern, the ERA kit was painted in desert yellow. Heavily weathered all over by sand
Iraq, May 2004

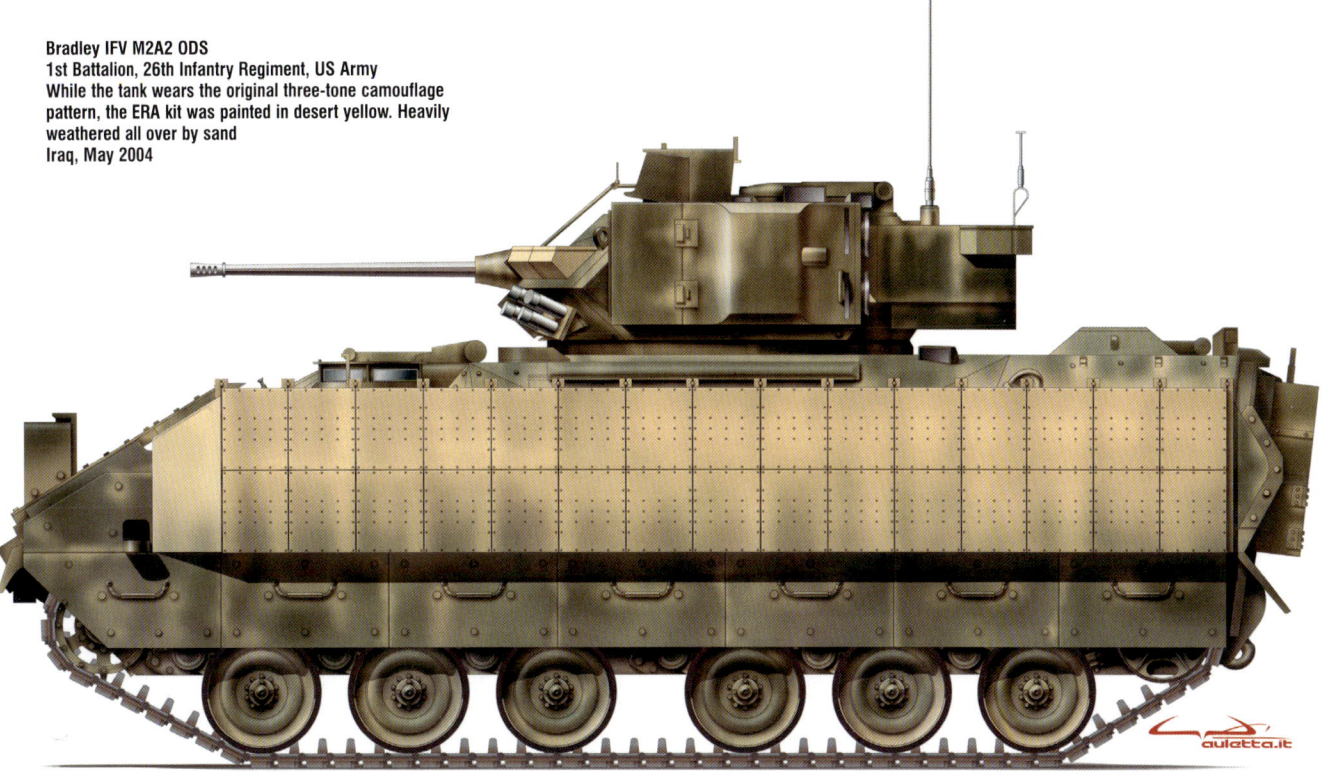

Bradley IFV M2A2 ODS
1st Squadron, 4th Cavalry Regiment, US Army
Fitted with the ERA Kit
North of Bayji, Iraq, 2004

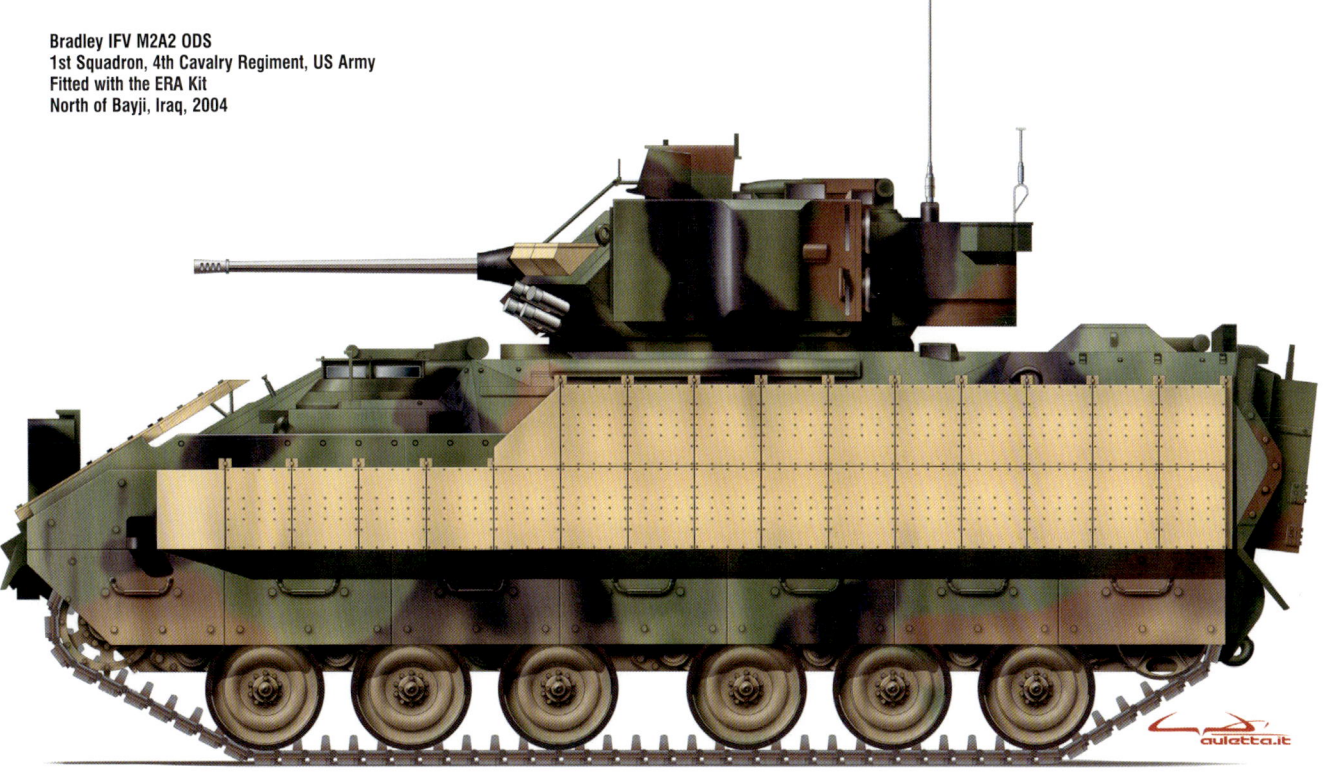

Bradley IFV M2A2
1st Battalion, 26th Infantry Regiment, US Army
This was one of the mixed Bradley fleet of the 26th IR
displayed in Iraq with different ERA kits

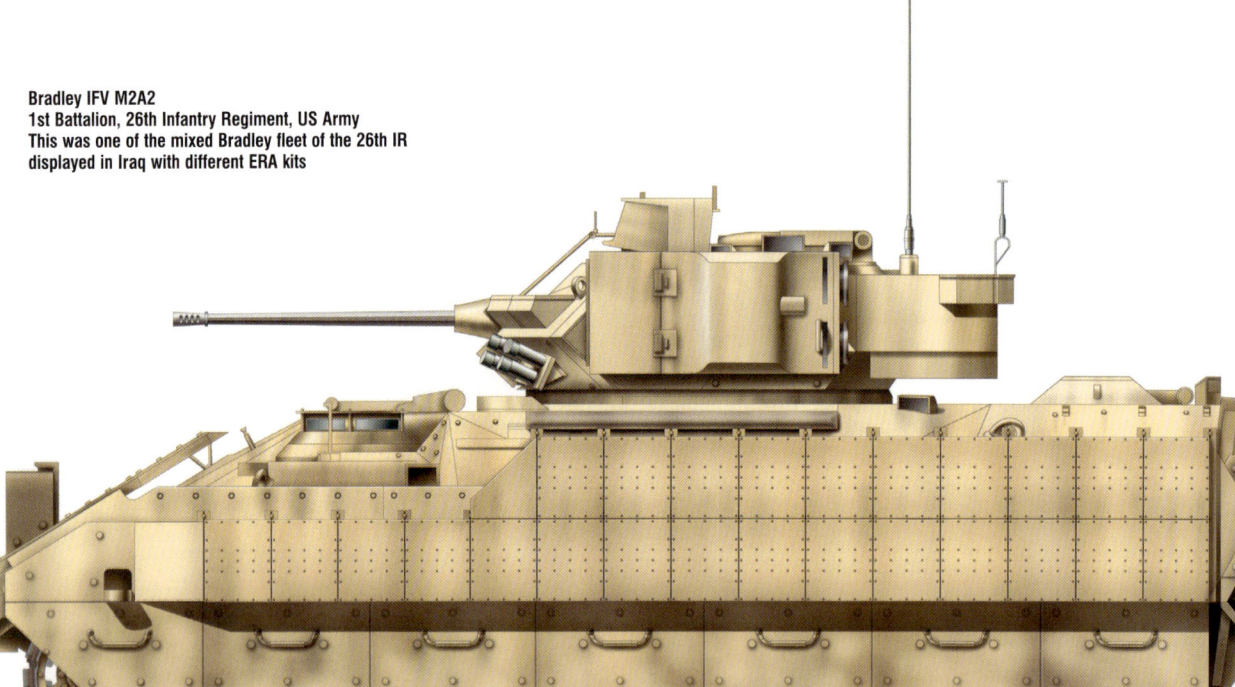

Bradley IFV M2A2 ODS
1st Battalion, 22nd Infantry Regiment, 4th Infantry Division,
US Army
Originally seen in Iraq without ERA kits, it operated in the
Bayji Region

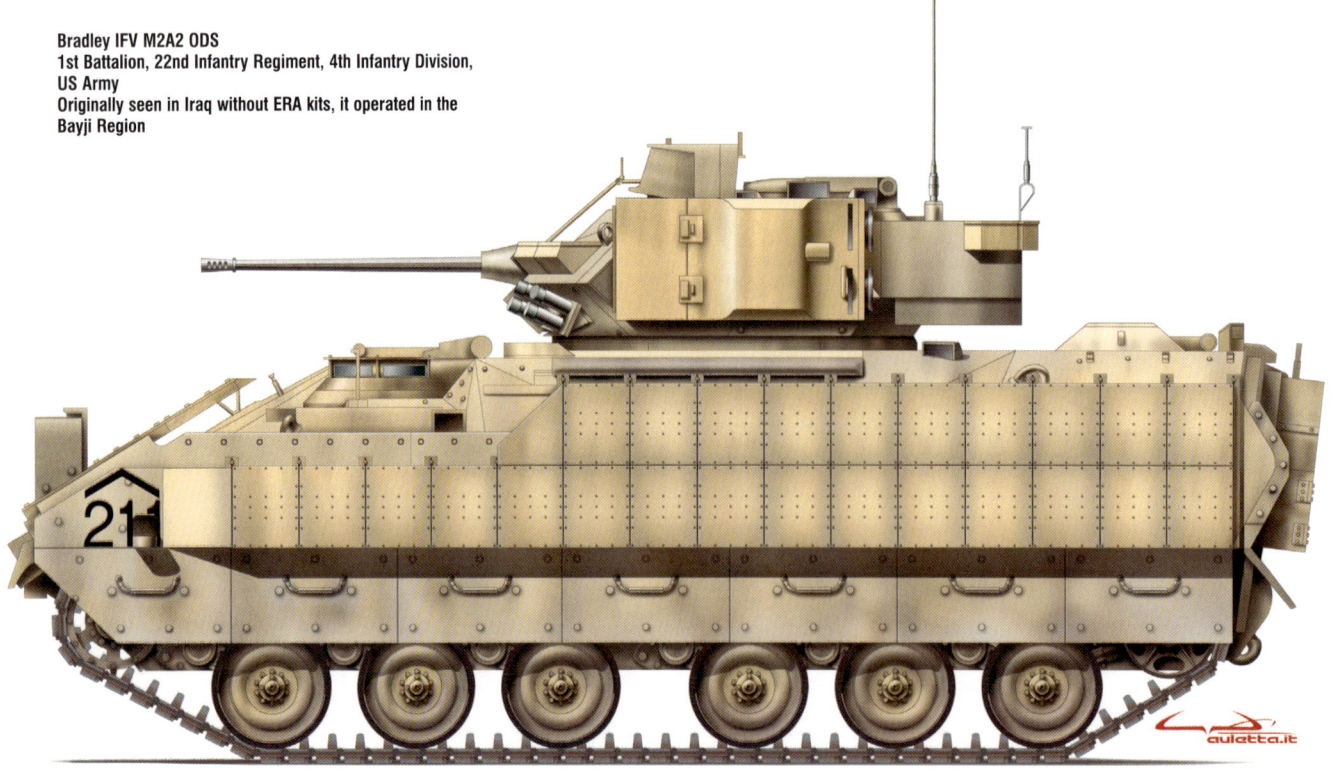

Bradley IFV M2A2 ODS
C Company, 1st Battalion, 8th Infantry Regiment, US Army
Like all of the vehicles of the 4th Infantry Division, it wears
the standard US Army desert camouflage.
Samarra area

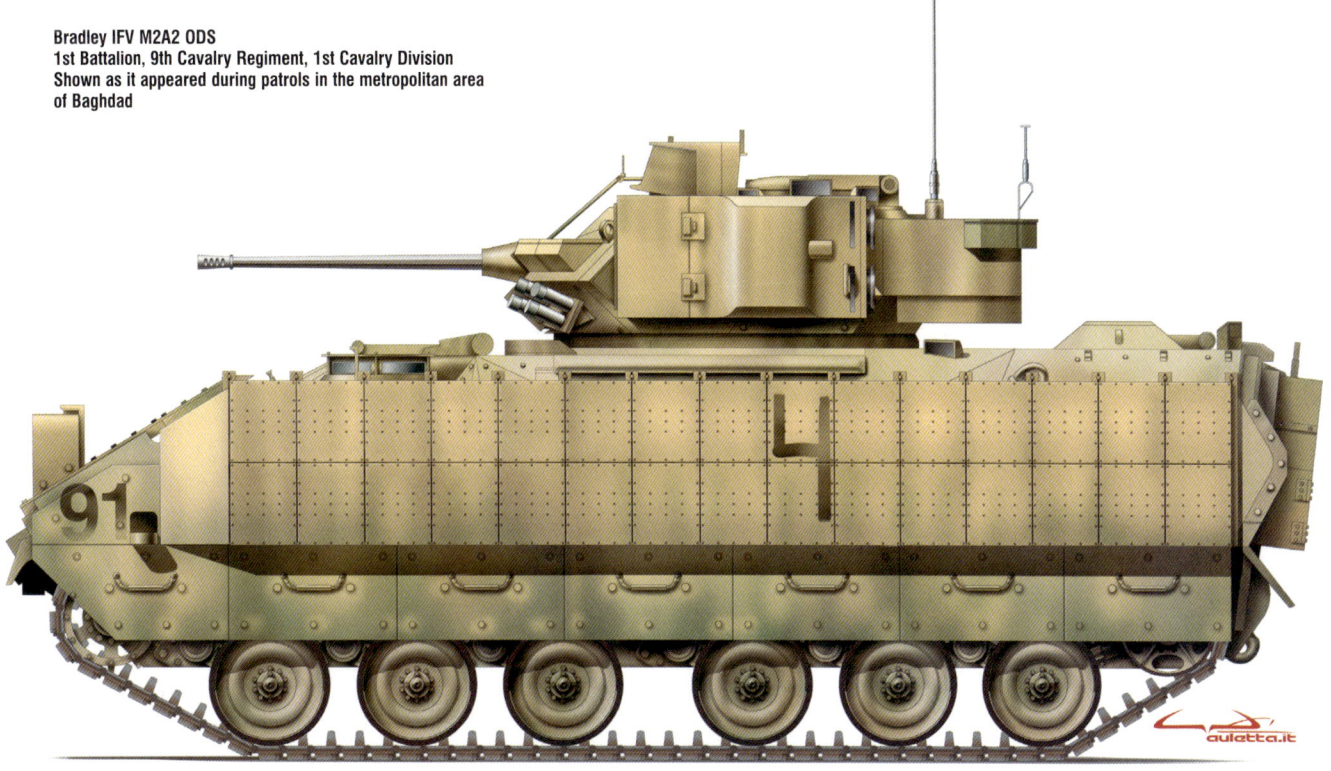

Bradley IFV M2A2 ODS
1st Battalion, 9th Cavalry Regiment, 1st Cavalry Division
Shown as it appeared during patrols in the metropolitan area
of Baghdad

2 Modelling the Bradley M2A2 with ERA

by Andy Renshaw

I t's hard to imagine that a vehicle that has served in the US Army for almost thirty years is still in front line service. A constant evaluation and update program has kept the M2/M3 Bradley 'state-of-the-art' with both internal and external changes to compensate with the ever changing face of modern warfare. Tamiya was quick to produce a kit of the M2 and M3 (with the M3 having a full interior) that was originally tooled for motorisation. Tamiya then released a M2A2 in the 1990's using the same hull and sprues but included new parts for the armour panels. At some point during its early years Academy released the Tamiya M2 and M3 under its own label, so now both companies have produced a M2A2 ODS; however the base moulds are still the old M2 and M3 Bradley kits!

So, much like the full size Bradleys, some work will be involved to update either kit to a current M2A2, and even more work will be required to build an M2A3. If you wish to do an M3A2 or A3, you will be in for some scratch-building as no kit builds into a M3 variant out of the box. Between the Academy and Tamiya offerings, it is Tamiya who are closest to an earlier M2A2 ODS as used during and shortly after the start of OIF, while the Academy kit reflects some later changes, such as hull armour plates and the revised nose armour, so choose your kit accordingly.

Legend Productions have some fine resin upgrade and detail sets to add to either kit and they make the job of adding ERA blocks or converting to a M2A3 much easier. For this build, I chose to do a M2A2 with ERA blocks, and that had a mix of some early and later ODS features. Using the Legend combined set for the M2A3 and ERA block upgrade, plus bits from the M2/M3 detail set, and a few Eduard items, we can take care of the external modifications. The other area that needs major improvement is the suspension and drive sprocket. All of this is a hold-over from the kit's motorised past, and at best lacks detail, or in the case of the sprocket is completely wrong. There are several upgrade sets available, or the suspension can be taken from an MLRS kit. Legend also has some outstanding road wheels we will use to replace the kit ones. All of this will bring a base kit that is nearly thirty years old up to 2010 standards!

For this build, we used the Academy M2A2 'OIF' boxing. The kit builds into a decent late M2A2 'Desert Storm' (ODS) out of the box, however there are many items that need updating and detailing. Some of the issues are because the base of the kit is the old original M2 boxing done by Tamiya in the early 1980s. In fact, the kit sprues still have M2 parts on them! One could use the Tamiya M2A2 ODS boxing as well and go through most of the same steps as with the Academy kit.

I decided to use the M2A2 seen illustrated elsewhere in the book as a guide to build the model. Being a late ODS Bradley; it needed the revised nose armour, which is supplied in resin in the Legend M2A3 conversion kit. The Academy kit comes with this in plastic, however the resin parts are better detailed and appear to be more the correct size. One odd feature is the pair of moulded holes in the middle of the resin part. After attaching to the hull, fill these holes with some thick plastic and smooth over with putty.

Eduard provides some very useful detail sets for the Academy and Tamiya Bradleys. They are virtually interchangeable due to the kits sharing the same base moulds. Depending on what version and timeframe you wish to do, you can choose from a host of etch details. Eduard's sets provide many of the smaller items that Legend does not, including tool clasps, CIP panels, and other details.

After the upper hull surgery is complete, the non-skid surface can be applied. I used the same technique as with the rest of the builds (see the Abrams build for some good 'how to' shots). Sharp-eyed readers will note that the first pass with the non-skid didn't get everything it should have, and later pictures show the non-skid added around the driver's area and other positions. Time spent studying reference photos before and during a build pays off! The white areas along the hull sides are where the wading skirt was removed.

Here is the assortment of aftermarket items we will be using for this build. If you plan on doing a M2A2 w/ the ERA, you will need items from the Legend M2A3 conversion even if you don't plan on building an A3. The Legend M2/M3 detail set is excellent for any Bradley build, and provides some very nice parts for the headlights and a major correction for the rear. It also provides many parts to upgrade the M2A2 and M3A2 to the ODS standard.

One of the holdovers from using the old M2 moulds on both the Tamiya and Academy kits is that the wading screens are still moulded onto the hull. These appear as long bulges near the edge of the hull behind the side armour plates. The wading screens were removed from Bradleys shortly after Desert Storm, so must be removed from these kits to bring them up to OIF standard. I only removed the portions near the front, as the rear sections would be covered by stowed gear and not seen. Cut and grind out the bulges, replace with a strip of plastic at the same angle as the hull, and smooth with liquid putty.

When doing the non-skid, some panels are best done before they are attached to the hull. Here are the kit-provided rear overhead hatch, the turret hatch, and resin armour panels that all need the non-skid. Notice how the bolts were masked with a drop of liquid mask to keep them from getting the non-skid material attached to them. If you are careful, the size of the drop will form a nice circle around the bolt, replicating the small area around that doesn't get the non-skid treatment!

Moving back to the lower hull, the Academy kit needs some help to properly attach and align the upper hull. When Academy did their re-tooling of the Tamiya upper hull, they left out the poly-caps and posts for the upper hull to attach to the front, and the rear locating tab. Plus after the modifications to the rear, any remaining alignment tabs are lost. To fix this, and improve fit, some square plastic stock was glued along the hull sides. This not only gives a positive glue point between the upper and lower hulls, but also squares up the side armour skirts which have a slight tendency to bow inward. If using the Tamiya kit, these modifications are not necessary, but do help.

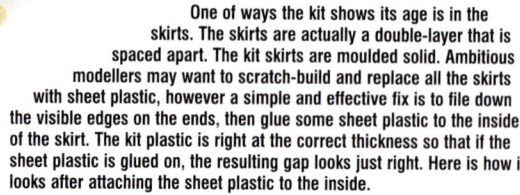

One of ways the kit shows its age is in the skirts. The skirts are actually a double-layer that is spaced apart. The kit skirts are moulded solid. Ambitious modellers may want to scratch-build and replace all the skirts with sheet plastic, however a simple and effective fix is to file down the visible edges on the ends, then glue some sheet plastic to the inside of the skirt. The kit plastic is right at the correct thickness so that if the sheet plastic is glued on, the resulting gap looks just right. Here is how it looks after attaching the sheet plastic to the inside.

The results from the outside can be seen here. A quick, but very noticeable improvement to an almost twenty-year old mould! Repeat this for all four ends. Note that on this particular vehicle, I removed the left front skirt to match my reference photos, so the now exposed end of the second skirt received this treatment.

This is a picture of the result of the Legend detail parts. Note how there are two, spaced metal panels behind where the rear stowage boxes will go. These are supported against the hull by small posts. The Legend set actually makes this easy to do, as the inside metal panel has etched holes that make the alignment of the posts, made of plastic rod, easy to do. Before you assemble the plates, use the ones with holes to mark the rod locations on the hull rear that you just built from plastic sheet. Drill holes on the marks the same diameter as the holes in the metal plate, thus also the same diameter rod you will use for the small posts.

To assemble the parallel plates, first make a small jig with three strips of plastic the thickness of the needed gap and attach these to a piece of scrap. Make sure the strips are spaced between the holes on the inner plate. Now lay the outermost plate face down, pushed against some type of straight-edge. Lay the jig with the strips across the plate, and then align the inner plate (the one with the holes) on top. Now you can insert small lengths of rod into the holes. Pre-cut the lengths longer than needed, dipping one end in super glue before inserting into the holes. Here in the pictures, one plate is complete, ready for the jig to be slipped out, while the next awaits assembly. Make sure you make mirror copies!

Here is another shot of the assembled rear. When attaching the metal plate assembly, trim the rods a little longer than needed, and slip them into the holes you drilled on the rear hull. You can now perfectly adjust the angle and distance the assemblies are from the hull, securing with glue once you're pleased with its position. When done with this, assemble the top and bottom hulls, and then you can add the resin ERA blocks for the hull sides at your leisure. A few bolts may need to be trimmed for a flush fit, but the resin ERA blocks line up perfectly with the bolt locations on the side armour plates.

The next item of major surgery is the rear. The Legend M2A2/A3 detail set provides some excellent parts to dress this area up, but it requires a bit of cutting and preparation. Removing all of the rear bulkheads that are behind the rear stowage boxes, these are then replaced with some thick plastic sheet. Cut the top portion oversize, and then once glued in they can be filed and trimmed to fit the upper hull perfectly. Go ahead and assemble the rear ramp and attach at this point. The resin parts on either side of the ramp replace the kit parts. Academy provide some acceptable parts in their kit, but the resin ones are nicer and are the correct size and shape.

With the hull assembled we can now start working on adding details. Here is the exhaust area. The brass screen came from the Legend detail set, with the details on the exhaust housing from Eduard. A small box was made with some scrap metal and inserted into the exhaust to form the actual tube, a detail missing from the kit.

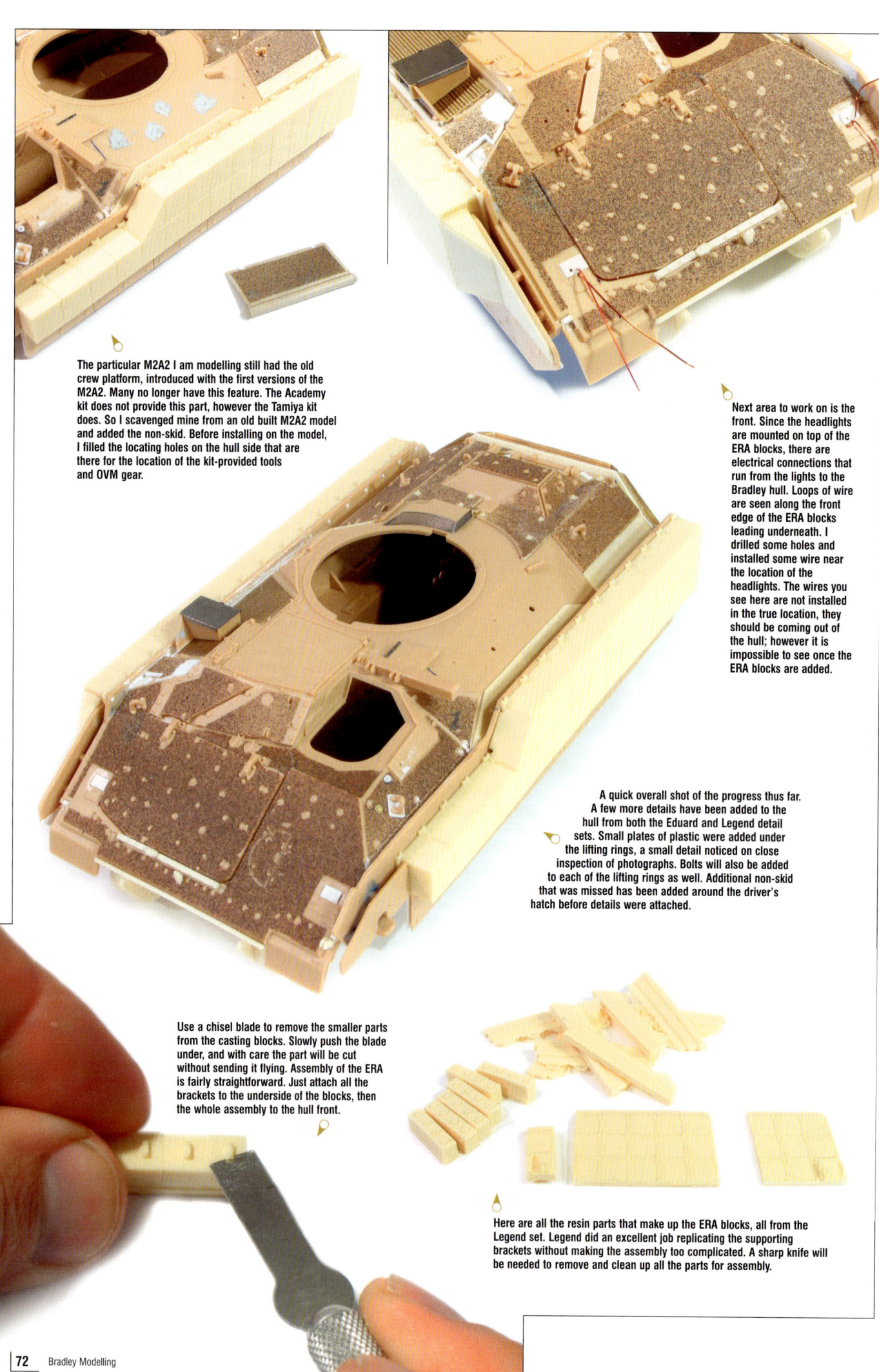

The particular M2A2 I am modelling still had the old crew platform, introduced with the first versions of the M2A2. Many no longer have this feature. The Academy kit does not provide this part, however the Tamiya kit does. So I scavenged mine from an old built M2A2 model and added the non-skid. Before installing on the model, I filled the locating holes on the hull side that are there for the location of the kit-provided tools and OVM gear.

Next area to work on is the front. Since the headlights are mounted on top of the ERA blocks, there are electrical connections that run from the lights to the Bradley hull. Loops of wire are seen along the front edge of the ERA blocks leading underneath. I drilled some holes and installed some wire near the location of the headlights. The wires you see here are not installed in the true location, they should be coming out of the hull; however it is impossible to see once the ERA blocks are added.

A quick overall shot of the progress thus far. A few more details have been added to the hull from both the Eduard and Legend detail sets. Small plates of plastic were added under the lifting rings, a small detail noticed on close inspection of photographs. Bolts will also be added to each of the lifting rings as well. Additional non-skid that was missed has been added around the driver's hatch before details were attached.

Use a chisel blade to remove the smaller parts from the casting blocks. Slowly push the blade under, and with care the part will be cut without sending it flying. Assembly of the ERA is fairly straightforward. Just attach all the brackets to the underside of the blocks, then the whole assembly to the hull front.

Here are all the resin parts that make up the ERA blocks, all from the Legend set. Legend did an excellent job replicating the supporting brackets without making the assembly too complicated. A sharp knife will be needed to remove and clean up all the parts for assembly.

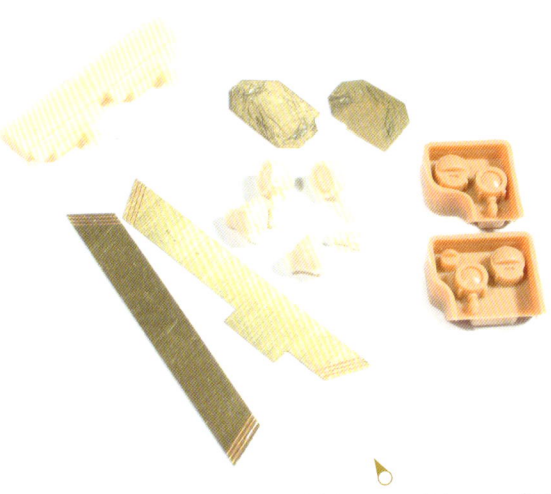

Once the ERA blocks are installed on the hull front, next will be the headlights. This is probably one of the largest detail improvements the Legend set provides. They are a little tedious and time consuming to assemble, however the end result is worthwhile. Annealing the brass by heating it red hot then letting it cool will soften it and make shaping easier. Here are all the components, and on the right are the kit parts.

With the headlight installed and the wires attached, we can now get a good look at the finished assembly. For added detail, use some smaller diameter wire and loop it several times behind the lights to replicate other electrical cables.

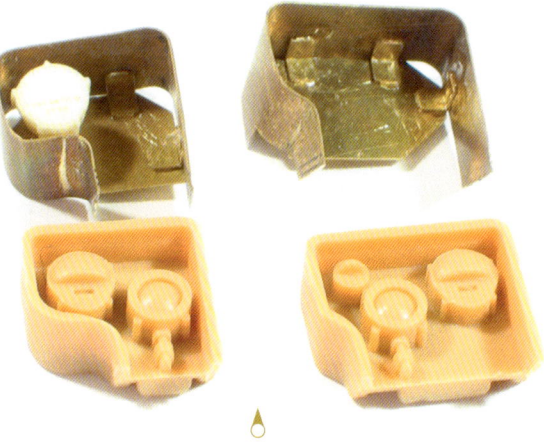

Detailed headlight assemblies at the top, kit parts along bottom. The difference is stark, even at this early stage of construction. Just the more realistic thickness of the metal and better-detailed resin components will make these catch eyes.

With the shroud assembled and turn signal light installed, we can attach them to the ERA blocks. Drill small holes for the headlight posts, as this will allow positioning the headlight at the best height within the headlight assembly. Note that the previously installed wire is now trimmed to size, wrapped in front of the blocks, and glued into position.

Moving on to the turret, a quick test fit of the resin armour panel showed that the moulded-on periscopes were going to be completely blocked by the thickness of the armour plate. So, next step would be to remove them and raise them to clear the armour plate. Also note that the kit sight housing, or 'dog house', has also been removed in anticipation of using the resin item supplied by Legend.

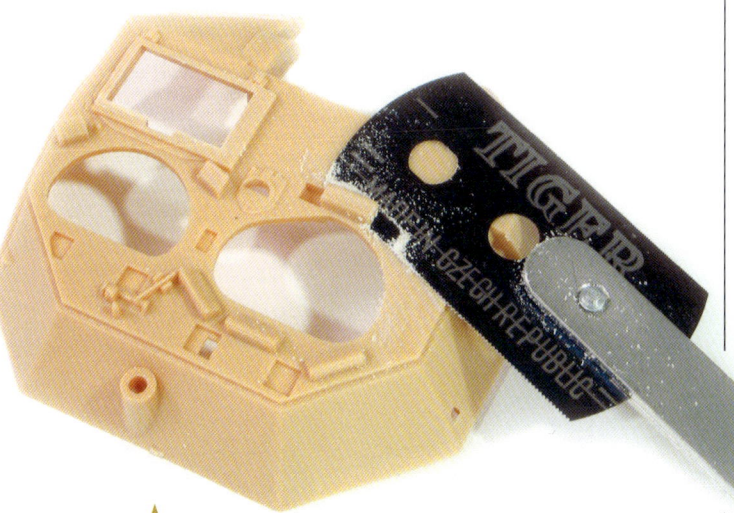

Here we are removing the periscopes with a super thin razor saw made by JLC tools. These are excellent tools and very high quality. This saw is very thin and so very little material is lost during cutting.

Once removed, all the periscopes were glued onto a piece of scrap plastic the same thickness as the armour plate. Once dry, each periscope was trimmed from the sheet, resulting in a perfect match to the kit part, then re-attached to the model.

Here the armour plate is installed in preparation for the assembly of all the turret parts. Note the small square of white plastic where the sight housing will go. Test fitting reveled that there would be a small gap here once the new housing was installed, and this plastic filled that gap.

The TOW launcher included in all 1:35 Bradley kits is the old TOW-1 from the original moulding, which is only good for the M2 and M3, and needs to be updated for any later mark. The distinguishing characteristic of the TOW-2 launcher is being able to see the tube itself from the front. Also the underside of the launcher should be cut away and the tubes exposed there as well.

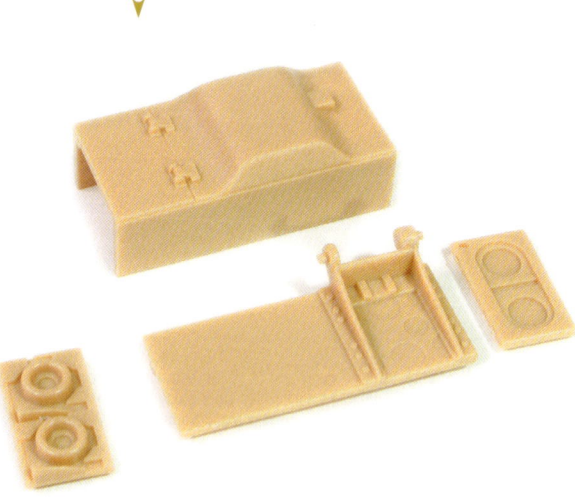

I discarded the kit's front replacing it with plastic having an oval cutout. It should be just wider than the diameter of the tubes. The tubes themselves were made of some aluminum stock which had the right thickness and diameter; however plastic could have worked as well. The tubes were spaced with some square stock and placed inside the launcher box. The bottom portion between the hinges was also removed, although with the launcher folded down this is barely seen.

Here is the launcher installed on the turret, which has had some more assembly done. The particular vehicle being modelled did not have the launcher cover, but if yours does be sure to round the bottom as the kit still has the old style cover from the early M2 and M3. It was also discovered that the armour plates on the turret are a bit too small, so some plastic square stock the same thickness was added to the edges of the armour plate to make them closer to the real size. Unmodified, some large gaps result between the armour panels that are very noticeable when comparing to reference photos.

Looking at the left side of the turret, the armour plates on this side were worse than the right. When doing this type of work, always glue on a larger than needed piece, and then trim after the glue has dried. This ensures an exact fit without having to do perfect measurements. The smoke grenade boxes are supplied by Legend, and are closer in size than those provided in the kit. The grenade launchers themselves needed some slight tweaking by making the top two tubes a wider angle.

The turret basket was replaced with sheet plastic, as this was easier than trying to thin and clean up the kit parts. It has been embellished with parts from Eduard and Legends. At first I installed a mix of early and later style ammunition can brackets, however I later made them all the same using the early style. Looking at the TOW-2 launcher, in hindsight I wish I had spent some time on the rear as well, as it should also be open around the tubes. I may still revisit that.

A final look at the turret with all of the details added, except the barrel. All of the light yellow resin came from Legend, while any silver metal is from the Eduard detail set. The grey plastic tie-downs on the rear turret slope, inside the basket, are extras from Dragon Sherman kits. Hatches were glued down with white glue so they could later be lifted and some crew figures added.

Two views of the completed turret with all its ephemera showing just how the addition of even the smallest amount of stowage enhances the look of the finished model.

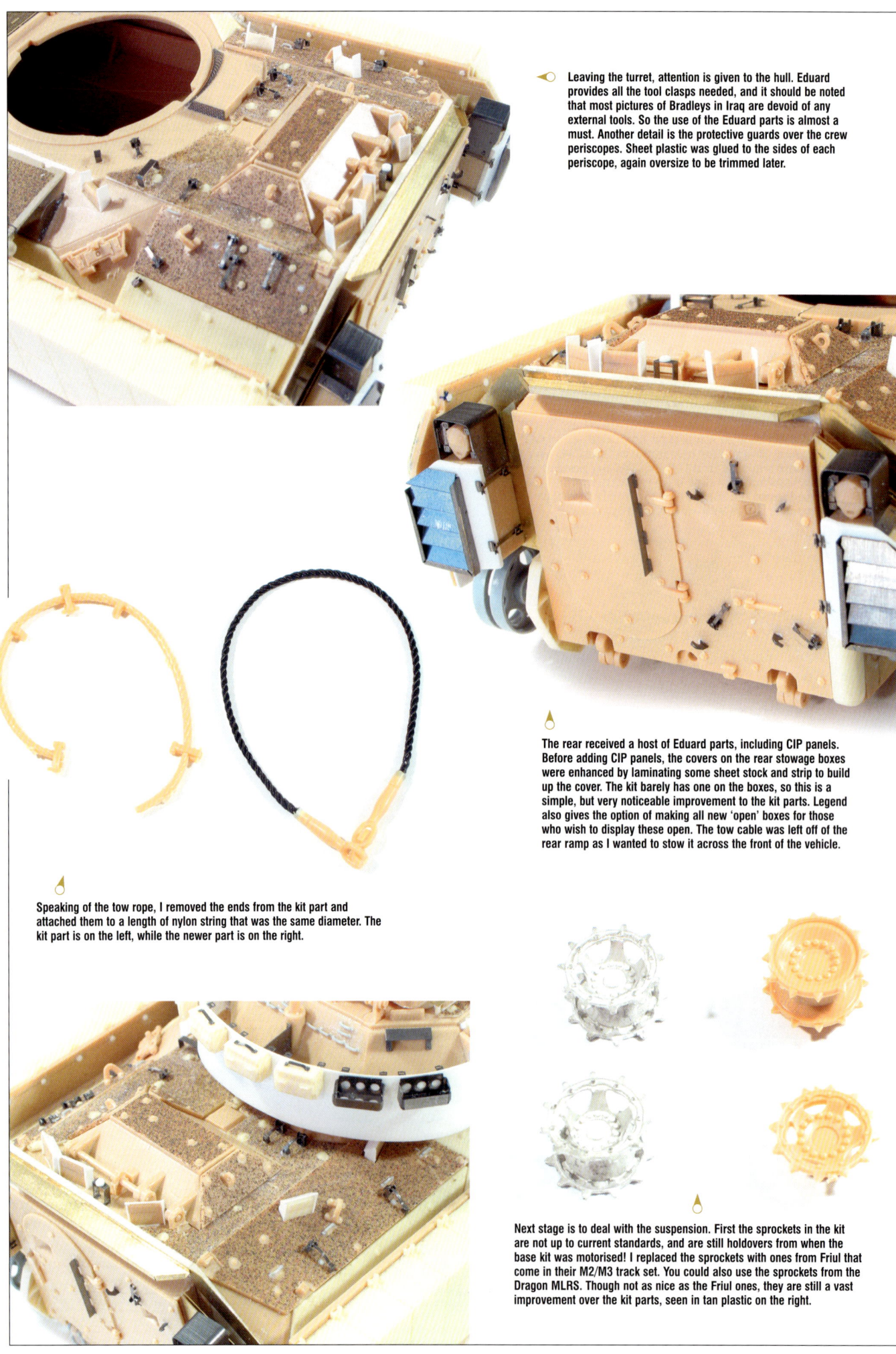

Leaving the turret, attention is given to the hull. Eduard provides all the tool clasps needed, and it should be noted that most pictures of Bradleys in Iraq are devoid of any external tools. So the use of the Eduard parts is almost a must. Another detail is the protective guards over the crew periscopes. Sheet plastic was glued to the sides of each periscope, again oversize to be trimmed later.

The rear received a host of Eduard parts, including CIP panels. Before adding CIP panels, the covers on the rear stowage boxes were enhanced by laminating some sheet stock and strip to build up the cover. The kit barely has one on the boxes, so this is a simple, but very noticeable improvement to the kit parts. Legend also gives the option of making all new 'open' boxes for those who wish to display these open. The tow cable was left off of the rear ramp as I wanted to stow it across the front of the vehicle.

Speaking of the tow rope, I removed the ends from the kit part and attached them to a length of nylon string that was the same diameter. The kit part is on the left, while the newer part is on the right.

Next stage is to deal with the suspension. First the sprockets in the kit are not up to current standards, and are still holdovers from when the base kit was motorised! I replaced the sprockets with ones from Friul that come in their M2/M3 track set. You could also use the sprockets from the Dragon MLRS. Though not as nice as the Friul ones, they are still a vast improvement over the kit parts, seen in tan plastic on the right.

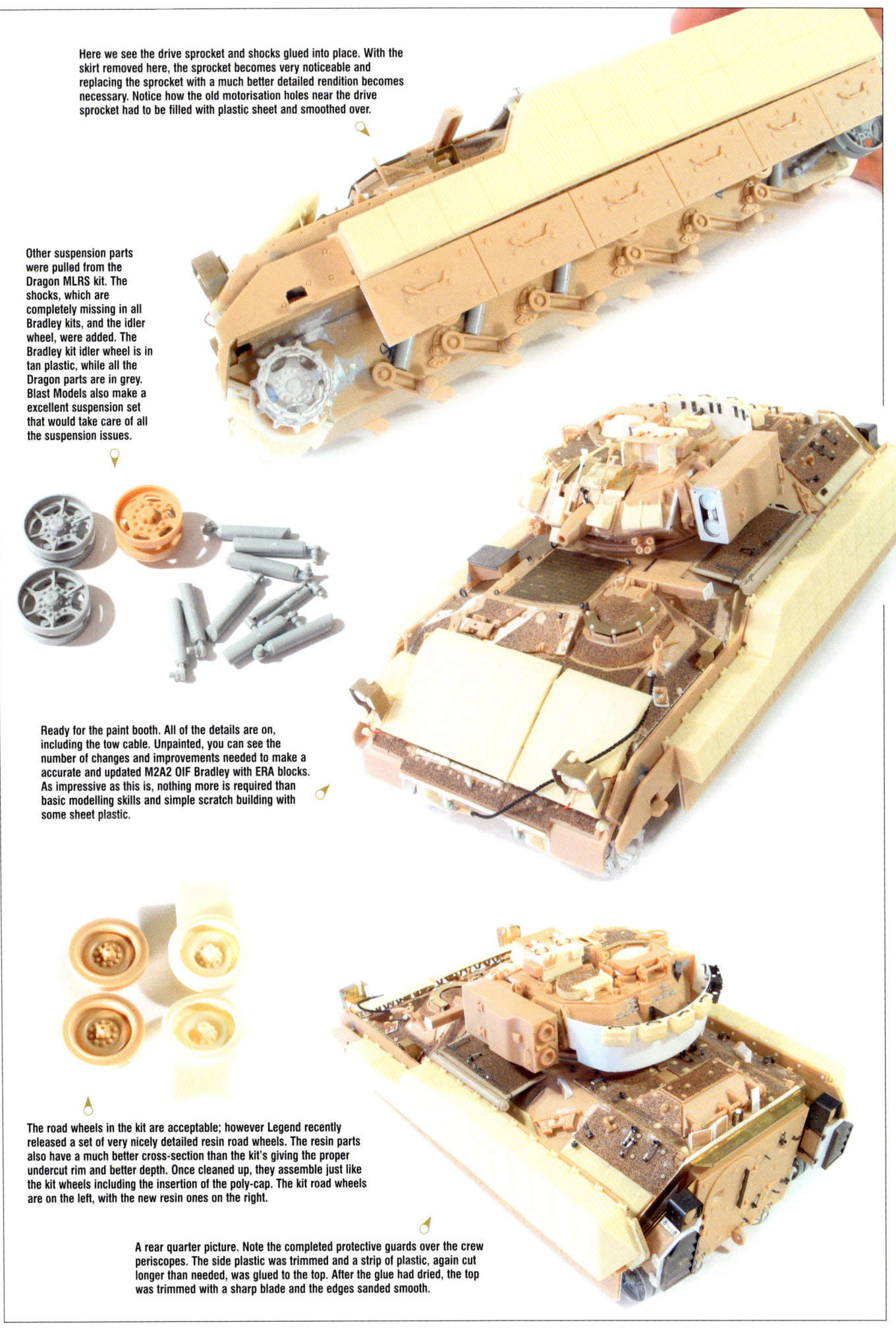

Here we see the drive sprocket and shocks glued into place. With the skirt removed here, the sprocket becomes very noticeable and replacing the sprocket with a much better detailed rendition becomes necessary. Notice how the old motorisation holes near the drive sprocket had to be filled with plastic sheet and smoothed over.

Other suspension parts were pulled from the Dragon MLRS kit. The shocks, which are completely missing in all Bradley kits, and the idler wheel, were added. The Bradley kit idler wheel is in tan plastic, while all the Dragon parts are in grey. Blast Models also make an excellent suspension set that would take care of all the suspension issues.

Ready for the paint booth. All of the details are on, including the tow cable. Unpainted, you can see the number of changes and improvements needed to make a accurate and updated M2A2 OIF Bradley with ERA blocks. As impressive as this is, nothing more is required than basic modelling skills and simple scratch building with some sheet plastic.

The road wheels in the kit are acceptable; however Legend recently released a set of very nicely detailed resin road wheels. The resin parts also have a much better cross-section than the kit's giving the proper undercut rim and better depth. Once cleaned up, they assemble just like the kit wheels including the insertion of the poly-cap. The kit road wheels are on the left, with the new resin ones on the right.

A rear quarter picture. Note the completed protective guards over the crew periscopes. The side plastic was trimmed and a strip of plastic, again cut longer than needed, was glued to the top. After the glue had dried, the top was trimmed with a sharp blade and the edges sanded smooth.

Even before paint, the model is looking impressive and 'a bit mean'. Lots of small details and improvements add up to make an outstanding model.

As with the other builds, I used the excellent Rust-Oleum dark grey automotive primer. Warm the can in hot tap water for five to ten minutes before spraying. Lightly spray on in coats, gradually building up coverage. Don't forget to turn the model to get the underside, and all possible angles. Focus first on the angles and the flat areas will get covered as a result. Let this dry for at least twenty-four hours.

Just to show it doesn't take fancy equipment to produce good models, here is a shot of my 'spray booth'. Using Vallejo acrylics allows me to spray inside, as there are no harmful fumes, although a face mask and an open window is always recommended. A simple cut-down cardboard box acts as a 'booth' to catch any overspray while airbrushing. Here I am putting on the first base colour over the primer.

For the base colour, I used Vallejo Model Air #71023 Hemp and #71040 Burnt Iron. I simply started with the Hemp, adding the Burnt Iron until I had a nice reddish brown hue. Spray in such a way that you build up layers of paint. Vallejo paint has an excellent translucent quality that if correctly utilised, can produce some truly stunning results. Spray lighter layers on the underside and in recesses, allowing the dark primer to 'show through' producing a pre-shade. Thoroughly cover the upper surfaces, as this will likewise become the pre-shade for the sand and other colours to follow.

Once the ERA blocks were dry, I masked off the edges to protect the sand coloured parts and sprayed the pale green. The green is a mix of Vallejo Model Air 71028 Sand with #71006 camouflage Light Green dripped in until it looked right. A little white was also added to lighten it up slightly. With no real paint match, I just used the photos as a guide, and kept in mind that subsequent weathering and washes was going to blend and darken the tone slightly.

Close examination of reference photos I was working from showed that the main body of the M2A2 was not the common 'sand' colour, but more of a pale green. The ERA blocks however were fully the sand colour. Using Vallejo Model Air 71028 Sand, I sprayed all the ERA blocks, again building up layers thus allowing some of the previous colour to show through.

At this point I started work on the tracks. The AFV Club tracks are outstanding, and a delight to use. They come in their own bag and require very little clean-up. Plus they snap together, making them very workable. The rubber pads on the outside are separate, so these were left off until after painting the tracks themselves.

Another shot of the model with the light green hull and tan ERA blocks. Note the dark green frontmost road-wheel. This was a small detail noticed on close inspection of the photographs.

To paint the tracks, I first primed them using the same primer used on the rest of the model. This is a very dark grey, so can replicate the rubber portions well (top). Next I used two strips of masking tape and masked off either side of the guide horns, the width of the inner rubber pads. The base track colour is from Vallejo's Panzer Aces line. I also dry-brushed on some Vallejo Light Tan colour. After removing the masks, we now have perfect tracks showing the clean rubber areas where the road wheels have made contact.

Another shot of the tracks installed. Be sure to not have any sag, as these are kept fairly tight. Note the end connector detail. The AFV tacks are absolutely beautifully detailed and add a lot compared to the kit rubber tracks, or even the metal ones from Friul. Do be sure, when installing, that the pads face the correct direction. I also didn't install any of the rubber pads until after putting the tracks on. The only pads installed are those that can be seen, thus none on the top or bottom run are on. No reason to!

Installing the tracks was fairly painless, and fitted over the Friul sprocket perfectly. Just feed them in from the rear, pulling them through the running gear with tweezers. Position the two ends along the bottom, remove any excess links, and snap the ends together.

With all the base colours on, we can start to work on weathering, details and variations. Looking at photos, the ERA blocks are a myriad of different shades. Vallejo's paints are excellent for slightly thinning, and using a brush laying on colour to tone underlying tones. Use light and dark tans, and even some greys to pick out different blocks, giving an almost chequerboard look. Be sure to always use photographs as a reference.

An up-close shot of some details after toning, washing, and dry-brushing. Note how subtle the effects are. Enough to make the details stand out, but not 'highlight' or 'outline' them, neither of which is seen on the real subjects. To do the wash and dry-brushing, the entire model was sprayed with Johnson's Klear (Future), then a thin wash of brown oil paint, with a touch of black, was added to all the recesses and around details. For dry brushing, an off white-very light tan oil paint was used. After it has all dried, if more contrast is needed, it can always be added with more wash and dry-brushing, layering the colour.

An overall shot of the model at this stage. More details have been added, such as the smoke grenades, barrel, and painting of headlights and tow cable. Next will be adding additional stowage and final details, plus additional weathering painting such as scratches and scuffs, then dusting with pigments.

This is a small pile of stowage to add to the Bradley. Most of this either came with the kit, or is found in the Legend Bradley stowage set. Note that at this stage of operations in Iraq, external stowage was kept at a minimum not only due to operating out of close bases, but also because anything external posed a fire hazard when hit by an RPG or IED. What is seen in the picture is more than what we will use. Best to have lots to choose from to best fit the model than to 'make do' with a few items. These also get the same wash and dry-brush techniques as the rest of the model.

Once the stowage was painted, I filled in the turret stowage box with various items, and used bits of tan coloured paper, a painted tea bag, and epoxy putty to fill in the gaps between the resin items. This gives it a more realistic 'filled-in' feel, than just a pile of resin bits.

On the front, a coil of barbed wire cast in resin from the stowage set was painted up. This was first coated with a dark grey, and then dry brushed with both silver and metallic colours to really make the wire stand out. With the final overall flat coat done, I painted the vision blocks with a Testors 'metallic dark red' and added some clear gloss to the lights.

Further weathering of the ERA blocks was done with Vallejo paint, slightly thinned and applied with a brush. Using the photographs as a reference, I added staining and streaking with a very light tan and browns.

For an overall dust effect, some light sand colour was mixed, thinned by 60%, and then sprayed on the bottom half of the model, including the tracks.

Another look at the stowage basket. Note here that items that would need to be easily accessed, such as water and food, are at the top, while bags and packs are buried. Everything is secured, and a few straps were added to create more detail.

Scratches on the corners and edges were first done in Vallejo light grey paint, and then some Model Master Metalizer 'steel' was dry-brushed and painted on with a fine brush but to a lesser degree than the light grey.

Some Vallejo rust colour pigment was then scrubbed into the top of the exhaust shroud. I used a cut down old brush for this, and its 'stubble shape' works great when working with pigments. Note the chalked 'X' on the front of the TOW tubes. This was a small detail noticed when zooming in on a high resolution photograph. It always pays to carefully study original photos!

Stepping back, the M2A2 is complete, and is a fine representation of an 'Operation Iraqi Freedom Bradley'.

3 The Stryker Infantry Fighting Vehicle

The Stryker emblem, painted on a 172nd SBCT Forward Op Base Marez, Mosul Iraq
(© US Army)

One of the icons of operation OIF is the Stryker family of vehicles. The development of the Stryker started in 2000 with a US Army joint contract to General Dynamics Corporation and General Motors, known as the GM/GDLS Defense Group. The timeline of development saw the attack of the World Trade Center and the opening stages of Operation Iraqi Freedom in early 2003 and by then the Stryker was in full stage testing and would have its baptism of fire by the end of that same year. The Stryker is designed to be an interim armored vehicle, standing between the heavy armour of the tanks, such as the M1 Abrams and Bradley fighting vehicles and the light armour such as the M113 and up-armored Humvee. Its purpose is not to replace either light or heavy armor, but provide a vehicle that can transport troops with speed, protection, and integration into the battlefield. Its unique capabilities have seen the US Army develop the dedicated 'Stryker Brigade Combat Team' (SBCT).

Breaking the tradition of naming armored vehicles after famous US Army officers and Generals, the Stryker is named after two enlisted posthumous Medal of Honor recipients Pfc Stuart S Stryker, who was killed near Wesel, Germany, March 24, 1945, and Spc4 Robert F Stryker, who died in the Vietnam War after shielding fellow solders from a claymore mine using his own body. It is most telling that the actions of those the vehicle is named after is reflected in the vehicle's performance itself as it shields mounted soldiers from IEDs, mines, and small arms fire, as well as having a moral boosting effect from its protection, speed, and endurance.

The Stryker Described

The 'Stryker' is a family of eight-wheeled, all-wheel-drive, armoured combat vehicles produced by General Dynamics Land Systems, and in use by the United States Army. The vehicle is based on the Canadian LAV III light-armoured vehicle, which in turn was based on the Swiss MOWAG Piranha III 8x8 and is the US Army's first new IFV since the M2/M3 Bradley of the 1980s. The Stryker was championed by General Eric Shinseki when he was US Army Chief of Staff, and currently the vehicle is employed in 'Stryker Brigade Combat Teams', light and mobile units based

Taken during their second Iraq tour, this 3/2 SBCT Stryker models the improved armour kit with blast panels along the top of the vehicle, angled down to deflect IED shrapnel. Note the Combat Identification Panel (CIP) along the front of the vehicle
(© US Army)

on the 'Brigade Combat Team Doctrine' that relies on vehicles connected by military C4I networks within the 'digital battlefield'.

Power Pack and Mechanical Features

All Strykers share common engine type, transmission, wheels, drive train components, and hydraulic systems. This makes the logistics of supplying basic parts easier and maintenance training less complex. Additionally, the power pack is a common Caterpillar diesel engine, the C7, which is used in many other US Army vehicles and trucks. This allows the use of common parts as US Army mechanics already have familiarity with the type. Designers strove to ease the maintainer's job, equipping most cables, hoses, and mechanical systems with quick-disconnecting mechanisms. The engine and transmission can be removed and reinstalled in approximately two hours, allowing repairs to the turbocharger and many other components to be done outside the vehicle. Pneumatic or hydraulic systems drive almost all of the vehicle's mechanical features, such as a pneumatic system that facilitates switching between 8X4 and 8X8 drive.

In addition to the common components, the M1130 and M113

also have an air-conditioning unit mounted as standard, plus there is a field retrofit for the other variants. The M1133 MEV also has a higher capacity generator to handle the increased electrical load of medical equipment.

Command, Control, and Targeting

Extensive computer support helps soldiers fight the enemy while reducing friendly fire incidents. Each vehicle can track friendly vehicles in the field as well as detected enemies. A day-night thermal imaging camera allows the vehicle commander to see what the driver sees. Soldiers can practice training with the vehicles from computer training modules inside the vehicle. The driver and the vehicle commander (who also serves as the gunner) have periscopes that allow them to see outside the vehicle without exposing themselves to outside dangers. The vehicle

A great view of an M1126 during a patrol. Note the water can racks attached to the lower slat armour panels and the camouflage netting over the rear of the vehicle. The netting not only provides some concealment from snipers, but also shade for the crew (© US Army)

CURRENT VARIANTS

There are ten different variants actively used by the US Army today. Of these, all of them have been deployed to Iraq. These are:

M1126	Infantry Carrier Vehicle (ICV)
M1127	Reconnaissance Vehicle (RV)
M1128	Mobile Gun System (MGS)
M1129	Mortar Carrier (MC-A and MC-B)
M1130	Command Vehicle (CV)
M1131	Fire Support Vehicle (FSV)
M1132	Engineer Support Vehicle (ESV)
M1133	Medical Evacuation Vehicle (MEV)
M1134	Anti-Tank Guided Missile Vehicle (ATGM)
M1135	Nuclear, Biological, Chemical, Reconnaissance Vehicle (NBC RV)

DEPLOYMENT

Currently there are seven Stryker Brigade Combat Team (SBCT) units, six of which at the time of writing have seen action in Iraq, with the last being deployed in Afghanistan in the summer of 2009

1st Brigade, 25th Infantry Division: October 2004 to Oct 2005. Reflagged as 2nd Stryker Cavalry Regiment

172nd Stryker Brigade Combat Team – 1/25 SBCT 'Arctic Wolves'; 16 Aug 05 – 03 Dec 06, reflagged in Dec 2006 as the 1st Stryker Brigade, 25th Infantry (redeployed in Sept 2008 – Sept 2009 as 1/25)

2nd Brigade, 25th Infantry Division, (SBCT) 'Warriors' Deployed Dec 2007 Task Force Lightning (returned March 2009, scheduled to deploy to Iraq summer 2010)

3rd Brigade, 2nd Infantry Division 'Arrowhead' – first Stryker Brigade formed. Deployed to Iraq: Nov 2003 – Nov 2004, late spring 2006 – Sept 2007. Deployed Aug 2009 – current

4th Brigade, 2nd Infantry Division 'Raiders' – reflagged from 2nd Armored Cavalry Regiment. Deployed May 2007 – June 2008, first use of MGS in Iraq. Deployed Sept 2009 – Current

5th Brigade, 2nd Infantry Division – 'Destroyers' final Stryker Brigade formed (deployed to Afghanistan July 2009)

2nd Stryker Cavalry Regiment (2SCR) – formed into SBCT in April 2005, reflagged from original 1st Brigade, 25th Infantry Division. Deployed in Aug 2007 – returned to Grafenwoehr, Germany Nov 2008

56th Stryker Brigade of the 28th Infantry Division, Pennsylvania National Guard Deployed to Iraq Jan 2009 – Sep 2009

Winning the hearts and minds of the Iraqi people?

A great shot illustrating the use of several types of Stryker vehicles, all from the 1/25 SBCT setting up a security checkpoint in 2004. In lower left, a M1130 CV with its extra antennas. Closest to the right is a M1127 RV, and behind it the M1126. Note the use of sandbags for additional protection from IED fragments *(© US Army)*

On patrol in July 2006, these Strykers show off the VLQ-12 'DUKE' ECM antennas. The DUKE system was developed by Syracuse Research Corporation to jam wireless IED detonation signals *(© US Army)*

Taken in Mosul, 2004, at least five Strykers are visible in this shot of the 1/25 SBCT in combat against insurgents. Two M1134 ATGM Strykers plus what is probably a M1133 are in the left most lane, while a M1126 takes position between the palms. A M1130 CV is in the foreground. Note the heavy use of sandbags along the top and IFF day-glo panels on each vehicle. The old truck in the background almost looks like a World War Two era German Opel! *(© US Army)*

Whereever soldiers travel, so shall the Jolly Roger! Soldiers from A company within the 172nd SBCT increase morale with a display of the skull and crossbones in Mosul during operations in 2006. Blast panels have been installed along the top of the Stryker. The rear panels fold down to facilitate the use of mounted weapons along the rear. Also note the use of the junk tire to soften the fall of the ramp *(© US Army)*

Another uncluttered shot showing more details of the slat armour and upper armour plate. This is the style of armour and slat provided by Griffon for 1:35 scale models *(© US Army, Dustin Senger)*

Here is the rear of the vehicle with the ramp down. No additional upper armour plates installed, as this picture was taken early in the Stryker's deployment, but a good look at the slat arrangement and jerry can racks, plus a glimpse at the interior *(© US Army)*

What powers the beast, a Caterpillar C7 turbo diesel that can generate 350 hp and almost 800 ft-lb of torque. From how clean this power pack looks it must be a brand new replacement *(© US Army)*

Up-close look at the headlights. These lights are mounted on extensions which are bolted onto the lift rings. These extensions raise the lamps above the slat armour to provide un-obstructed light. Some Stryker units have even mounted additional lamps and spotlights along the fronts of their vehicles

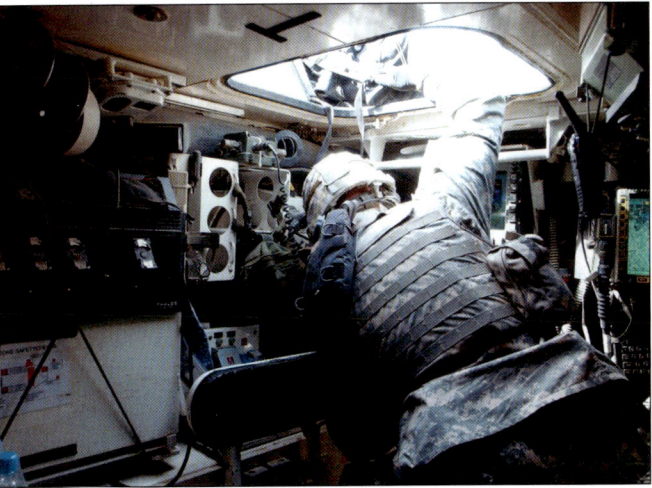

As this solder ducks down into the hatch of his Stryker, we get a glimpse of the interior. Of note is the GPS map display on the right. This resembles the multi-function displays used in aircraft and demonstrates how the Stryker is digitally integrated into the battlefield *(© US Army, Sgt 1st Class Steven Petibone)*

commander has almost a 360-degree field of vision; the driver, a little more than 90 degrees. General Dynamics Land Systems is developing a new Power and Data Management Architecture to handle computer upgrades.

Protection

The armour suite has been made thicker than the MOWAG design to stop 14.5 mm armour-piercing machine-gun rounds and artillery fragments. And the automatic fire extinguishing system has sensors in the engine and troop compartments that activate one or more Halon fire bottles, which can also be activated by the driver. 'Catchers' mask' – style deflectors known as 'slat armour' detonate explosive rounds at some distance from the hull. This type of armour is cheaper and lighter than spaced appliqué-plate reactive armour. The fuel tanks are externally mounted and designed to blow away from the hull in the event of

explosion. The CBRN (Chemical, Biological, Radiological, and Nuclear) Warfare system keeps the crew compartment airtight and positively pressurised. There are plans to add the 'Boomerang' anti-sniper system and Raytheon 'Quick Kill' anti-RPG system.

Mobility

The vehicle can alter the pressure in all eight tyres to suit terrain conditions: highway, cross-country, mud/sand/snow, and emergency. The system warns the driver if the vehicle exceeds the recommended speed for its tire pressure, then automatically inflates the tires to the next higher pressure setting. The system can also warn the driver of a flat tire, although the Stryker is equipped with run-flat tire inserts that also serve as bead-locks, allowing the vehicle to move several miles before the tire completely deteriorates. Unlike many modern armoured

personnel carriers, the Stryker is not an amphibious vehicle, but watertight combat hatch seals allow it to ford water up to the tops of its wheels.

The US Army plans to improve its Stryker vehicles with the introduction of improved semi-active suspension, modifications reshaping the hull into a shallow 'V-shaped' structure, with additional armour for the sides, redesigned hatches to minimise gaps in the armour, blast absorbing mine resistant seats (or benches), non-flammable tyres, an upgrade to the remote weapon station that allows it to fire on the go, increased 500 amp power generation, a new solid state power distribution system and data bus, and the automotive and power plant systems improvements to support a 25% gross vehicle weight increase. The upgraded V-hull will be part of the new 'StrykShield' situational awareness kit, which will address many of these upgrades.

As already noted there are eight configurations of Stryker, including the M1135 nuclear, biological, chemical reconnaissance vehicle (NBC RV); M1134 anti-tank guided missile (ATGM);

101st Airborne leadership carries on a conversion with the crew of this MGS. Modellers will want to note the weathering on the vehicle, as well as the uniforms and equipment of the soldiers
(© US Army, Maj John Paul Arnold)

A pair of slat armoured Strykers on patrol in Iraq
(© US Army)

Another picture of a 4th Brigade Stryker in Baqubah, Iraq, May 2007. Note the additional armoured cupola around the commander's station. Also this particular vehicle has a MK19 40mm grenade launcher installed
(© US Army, Sgt Armando Monroig)

A very interesting picture showing a M1134 ATGM with a SPARK, or Self Protective Adaptive Roller Kit. Though not standard fit for a M1134, and more common on an ESV, this shows that in the combat zone, anything goes if it works and gets the mission done'

The M1133 MEV is the medical version of the Stryker. It has a higher troop compartment, air conditioning, and more powerful generators. Note the extended slat armour along the top rear to accommodate the taller troop compartment and the Red Cross signs. These signs are hinged so they can be hidden from combatants that may not respect the symbol and use it as a point of aim
(© US Army, Dustin Senger)

Uncluttered with gear, this M1126 gives us a good look at the front slat armour arrangement and other details. Note the strobe flasher light. Slat armour adds an additional 7,000 lb of weight to the 38,000 lb vehicle *(© US Army)*

Loading onto a flatbed, a Stryker gives us a good shot of the underside. Note the CIP and the various foot loops and handles added to the slat armour. The CIP was developed directly from experience in Desert Storm where there was an excess of Friendly-Fire incidences. The CIP shows up in thermal sights as a slightly cooler, or different colour, square on the surface of the vehicle marking it as 'friendly' *(© US Army)*

An M1134 ATGM of the 172nd SBCT makes its way through a rain soaked street of Mosul. The ATGM is equipped with a dual TOW launcher that uses the BGM-71 TOW-2 family of missiles *(© US Army, Maj David Albano)*

This 2/25 M1134 was taken in 2008. It is interesting as it shows the addition of armoured glass cupola and a different style of lower armour over the wheels. Note the traffic cones tucked in the front and the slat armour that appears to be missing from the side hatch *(© US Army, Sgt Jacob Smith)*

The 56th SBCT is the only National Guard Stryker unit, and was deployed to Iraq in 2009. This shot of elements of the 56th on patrol give a good look at a current Stryker. Armoured glass panels have been added around the hatches and the rear of the vehicle, plus there is a full complement of ECM and anti-IED devices fitted. Also note the extra flood lamps added to the front (© US Army)

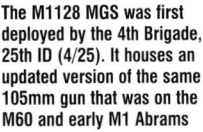

The M1128 MGS was first deployed by the 4th Brigade, 25th ID (4/25). It houses an updated version of the same 105mm gun that was on the M60 and early M1 Abrams (© US Army)

M1133 medical evacuation vehicle (MEV); M1129 mortar carrier (MC); M1132 engineer squad vehicle (ESV); M1130 command vehicle (CV); M1131 fire support vehicle (FSV); and the M1127 reconnaissance vehicle (RV). They have parts commonality and self-recovery abilities and are equipped with a central tire-inflation system. The reconnaissance vehicle is fitted with the Raytheon long-range advanced scout surveillance system (LRAS3). The system includes a second-generation horizontal technology initiative (HTI) thermal imager, day TV and eyesafe laser rangefinder. The US Army is to enhance the system by lengthening the sensor mast to 10m, increasing the range to 10km. The first of 17 LRIP nuclear, biological, chemical reconnaissance vehicle (NBC RV) variants was delivered in December 2005 and its systems can collect and automatically integrate contamination information with vehicle navigation and meteorological sensor data and then transmit digital warning messages to other forces.

M1126 Infantry Carrier Vehicle (ICV)

The M1126 is the basic infantry carrier vehicle (ICV) and provides armoured protection for the two-man crew and a squad

It's not all dry sand in Iraq. This Stryker rolls through the mud while being directed to a staging location (© US Army)

of nine infantry soldiers. The basic hard steel armour is augmented by appliqué panels of lightweight ceramic/composite armour. The armour provides integral all-round 14.5mm protection against machine gun rounds, mortar and artillery fragments. As protection against rocket-propelled grenades (RPGs), Stryker vehicles deployed to Iraq are outfitted with a 'cage' of slat armour, which encircles the vehicle about twenty-four inches from the main body. In March 2005, BAe Systems was awarded a contract to provide 289 full-vehicle add-on reactive armour kits for the Stryker, to be delivered between September 2005 and October 2006. So far these have not shown up in combat deployed units. The ICV has an M151 Protector remote weapon station (RWS), with a universal soft mount cradle, which can mount either a 0.50-caliber M2 machine gun, MK19 40mm grenade launcher or MK240 7.62mm machine gun. It is also armed with four M6 smoke grenade launchers. In August 2005, a TIM1500 640×480 uncooled thermal imaging camera for the remote weapon station was also ordered. The vehicle's commander has an FBCB2 digital communications system that allows communication between vehicles through text messaging and a map network, as well as with the battalion. The map shows the position of all vehicles on the battlefield and the commander can mark the position of enemy forces on the map which can then be seen by other commanders. FBCB2, 'the tactical internet', includes the Raytheon AN/TSQ-158 enhanced position location reporting system (EPLRS).

M11127 Reconnaissance Vehicle (RV)

The RV is supplied to the Reconnaissance, Surveillance, and Target Acquisition (RSTA) troop platoons and infantry battalion scout platoons. The RV carries a five-man reconnaissance team and it mounts a .50cal MG. The RV can deliver a scout and relay information. Mounted to the side of the commander's hatch are a Long-Range Advanced Scout Surveillance System (LRAS3) pod, a real-time acquisition, target detection, recognition, identification, and far-target location collection system. It has stand off, all-weather collection sensors and includes a forward-looking infrared thermal imager, a day video camera, laser rangefinder, long-range common aperture reflective optics, and a GPS interferometer subsystem.

The camouflage netting carried by this Stryker not only affords protection from insurgents, but also relief from the heat! (© US Army)

M1128 Stryker Mobile Gun System

Eight pre-production Stryker Mobile Gun Systems were delivered between July 2002 and March 2003, and the MGS entered service with the US Army in May 2007, with the first operational deployment to Iraq with the 4th brigade, 2nd Division. By November 2007, three Stryker brigades had received the MGS. The Stryker MGS was also selected by the Canadian Army, which plans to acquire some sixty-six examples systems to replace Leopard 1 tanks. However it was decided to acquire surplus Leopard 2 tanks instead. The Stryker mobile gun system variant consists of the basic vehicle with a General Dynamics Land Systems fully stabilised shoot-on-the-move low-profile turret, which is fitted with an M68A1E4 105mm cannon with muzzle brake and an M2 0.50-calibre commander's machine gun. The Stryker MGS has on board eighteen rounds of 105mm main gun ammunition, 400 rounds of 0.50-calibre ammunition and 3,400 rounds of 7.62mm ammunition, and also a pair of M6 smoke grenade launchers is fitted. The mobile gun system has the same

Soldiers with 73rd Engineers Co with the 1st SBCT, 25th ID out of Alaska looked quite pleased with their M1132 Engineer Support Vehicle. The ESV can have various attachments on the front including blades and mine plows depending on the mission. They are also equipped with automatic lane markers on the rear of the vehicle that drop as the path is cleared
(© US Army, Spc Opal Vaughn)

Plenty of scope here for the super-detailer, as this Stryker carries a plethora of items on its hull (© US Army)

An M1134 TOW-armed M1143 ATGM Stryker on patrol *(© US Army)*

'Fire in the Hole'! *(© US Army)*

Firing a mortar onto enemy positions at night is a true spectacle *(© US Army)*

A Stryker ICV with foot soldiers on the streets of Iraq *(© US Army)*

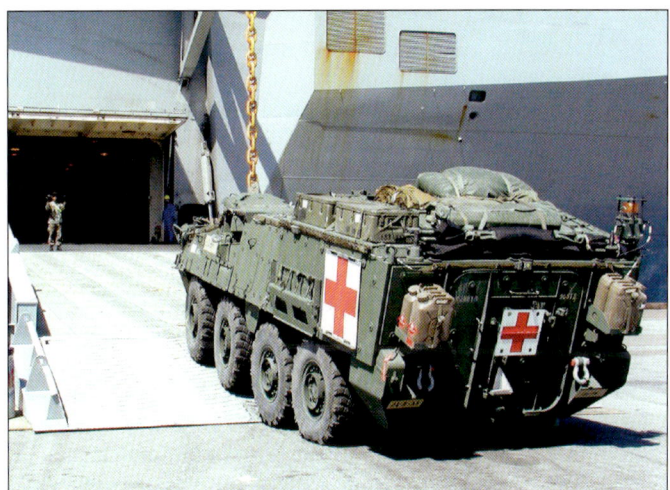

Unarmed MEVs allow for the evacuation of casualties over rough terrain

A Stryker ESV with Pearson V blade Surface Mine Clearance Device (SMCD) or Surface Mine Plough (SMP)

Cresting a hill, this ESV shows the bottom of the SPARK mine roller attached to the Joint Fitting Kit (JFK)

The MEV vehicle carries a trauma specialist

C4ISR communications and driver's vision equipment as the ICV, but the gunner has three periscopes and a compact modular sight with dual field of view day and thermal channels. The MGS also has detectors for nuclear, biological and chemical weapons.

Although the M1128 could be viewed as a tank, it is far from it merely sharing some tank-like features. An advantage to the brigade combat teams in having the mobile gun vehicle of the same Stryker family of vehicles is the commonality across the entire capability and the reduced logistics requirement. The Stryker mobile gun does not require a track-vehicle mechanic. The vehicle is fast, maneuverable, quiet and accurate, and is one of the most lethal ground vehicles for the urban environment such as can be found in Iraq today. The Stryker's sensors give the US soldiers a real edge against guerrillas on the night missions as these systems extend the 'eyes' of the troops further than conventional NVG's. Also the MGS's variety of weaponry is attractive, from machine guns that can fire single warning shots to high-explosive rounds that can flatten a building. One canister round fires a spread of anti-personnel steel balls from the turret like an enormous shotgun, and as such is very welcome when overwhelmed with an opposing force of insurgents.

M1129 Mortar Carrier (MC-A and MC-B)

To provide the units with a mobile source of indirect fire, the M1129 Mortar Carrier was developed. The early version, MC-A, was a lightly modified M1126 that had provisions to carry two mortars, crew, and ammunition. The mortar team would arrive in position, then dismount the vehicle and set up the mortars outside the vehicle. Obviously not the ideal situation for combat, especially in a mobile, asymmetric style warfare recently experienced, the MC-B was developed. The Mortar Carrier B has a highly modified hull with vertical sides and large overhead hatches. The 120mm mortar is mounted in a recoil system and

can be fired from within the vehicle itself by opening the top hatches. The suspension system was also reinforced. Onboard computer and fire control systems link the vehicle and team up to the 'digital battlefield' where they can receive, calculate, and coordinate fire missions while on the move between positions.

M1130 Command Vehicle (CV)

The M1130 is essentially the mobile battlefield command post for commanders to coordinate and control the movement of their troops. The CV is very similar to the M1126, however is full of gear and communications equipment for the command role. It comes in six configurations, including: Brigade Commander Command Vehicle, Battalion Command Vehicle, S3 TAC Command Vehicle, RSTA Squadron Command, Battalion S3, and the Tactical Air Control Party for the US Air Force.

M1131 Fire Support Vehicle (FSV)

The FSV acquires, identifies, and reports distant targets to the artillery battalion and the mortar elements. The vehicle's Fire Support Sensor System (FS3) has an AN/TAS-4B thermal imager/day camera, laser rangefinder, and AN/TVQ-2 laser locator designator for use with laser-guided smart munitions. Targeting data collected by the FSV is shared through four radio nets.

M1132 Engineer Squad Vehicle (ESV)

The ESV is deployed with supporting Engineer Companies within the SCBT. The ESV is equipped with hydraulic and electrical fittings on the front that can mount any number of fittings including: Surface Mine Plow, Lightweight Mine Roller, Angled 'V' Mine Plow, or the straight obstacle blade. The ESV can likewise be equipped with Lane Marking Equipment dispensers along the rear, to mark the lane as it is cleared of mines. Also at the disposal of the company is various other equipment including the M58A4

Stryker Fire Support Vehicle on patrol

The ATGM Stryker is an anti-armour and assault weapon and carries a GDLS remote TOW turret

With both Iraq and Afghanistan being more arid climates, trials have begun with painting Strikers in a CARC tan similar to that used on the M1A2 Abrams and Bradley (© US Army)

Air mobility was a requirement during the Stryker program. Being able to load an unmodified Stryker onto a transport aircraft means that it can also be deployed within minutes of being driven off, thus providing armour for a quick reaction force. Here a Stryker is loaded onto a C-17 Globemaster III
(© US Army, Staff Sgt Robert Barney)

MCLIC, or Mine Clearing Line Charge, and mine dispensers to perform both mobility and counter-mobility operations.

M1133 Medical Evacuation Vehicle (MEV)

Unarmed MEVs allow for the evacuation of casualties over rough terrain. The vehicle carries a trauma specialist, and four stretcher patients, or six sitting or two litter and three sitting patients. The right three-quarters of the rear compartment, behind the commander's hatch has been built up by ten inches and overall the compartment is wider. This means that the slat armour has been modified by being wider toward the rear and having additional raised panels. Storage inside the vehicle provides all the basics for first responder triage of wounded and minor surgical instruments. Also the MEV is equipped with the MC4 Medical Communication for Combat Casualty Care which includes a database with medical records and tracking.

M1130 patrols near Rawah, Iraq as a deterrence force against foreign fighters from entering Iraq. The tow bar has been lashed down to the top of the slat cage. The slat armour is the same for the M1126, M1127, M1130, M1131, and M1134 while the M1132, M1133, and M1135 have slight differences. The M1128 has a much different rear and modified sides to clear the turret *(© US Army)*

A great picture of a pair of dusty Strykers. Of interest is the installation of a second DUKE ECM antenna, and some type of stowage box along the side on top of the slat armour. The foremost vehicle also mounts a MK 19 40mm grenade launcher. There is also a rotating beacon mounted on the left side on top of the slat
(© US Army)

M1134 Antitank Guided Missile Vehicle (ATGM)

The ATGM Stryker is an anti-armor and assault weapon and carries a GDLS remote TOW turret above the centre of the rear compartment containing a pair of TOW-2B missile tubes, a thermal imager and day video camera, all in an armored pod. There are also four four-tube M6 grenade launchers mounted and a M240B machine gun is also carried.

M1135 NBC Reconnaissance Vehicle (NBCRV)

The NBRCV is fitted with an overpressure system that maintains a higher internal air pressure than exterior air pressure to prevent NBC agents from infiltrating the vehicle. An integrated NBC sensor suite and meteorological system is carried that includes a chemical agent detector and M21 remote sensing chemical agent alarm.

Tan coloured – Desert Bound

More than six years after sending the first Stryker armoured vehicles into desert combat, the Army finally decided that it's probably a good idea to start painting them tan so they will blend in with the environments in Afghanistan and Iraq! As one spokesman commented 'Strykers will blend into surroundings better as they are now less likely to stand out like silhouettes.' Since 2003, Stryker units deploying to Iraq have done so with their vehicles painted in deep green, while most other units deployed with tan vehicles. The 5th Stryker Brigade, from Fort Lewis, Washington was amongst the first to deploy to Kandahar and Zabul in 2009 with its vehicles painted tan.

This 172nd SBCT M1133 MEV sits in an open wheat field in support of a joint US Army and Iraqi police search and destroy mission. Note that the Red Cross panels have been folded over, plus the amount of stowed gear. The extended upper slat panels can also be seen to good effect (© US Army)

The wetter, the better? Rolling through partially flooded streets on patrol in February of 2006. The smoke discharge tubes on the CWS are fitted with a hodgepodge mix of smoke grenades (light green) plugs (black) and others are left empty. The crew has also stacked a blue cooler and traffic cones on the roof (© US Army)

3   Stryker Walkaround

The vehicle is based on the Canadian LAV III light-armoured vehicle, which in turn was based on the Swiss MOWAG Piranha III 8x8 *(© Hans-Hermann Bühling)*

Looking to the rear of the .50cal *(© Hans-Hermann Bühling)*

The XM151 Remote Weapons Station with .50cal and grenade launchers *(© Hans-Hermann Bühling)*

Close-in on a headlamp (© Hans-Hermann Bühling)

Self-recovery Rotzier Triebmatic powered winch (© Hans-Hermann Bühling)

Close-in on the M6 smoke grenade dischargers (© Hans-Hermann Bühling)

Front sloping aspect showing non-slip surface (© Hans-Hermann Bühling)

Driver's mirrors and tow-bar
(© Hans-Hermann Bühling)

Hatch to driver's compartment *(© Hans-Hermann Bühling)*

Remote sensor *(© Hans-Hermann Bühling)*

Winch cable drum and location of pioneer tool rack on a M1129 Mortar Carrier
(© Hans-Hermann Bühling)

Side stowage boxes on a M1135 NBCRV *(© Hans-Hermann Bühling)*

Rear door open, and showing the DWSS Double Wheel Sampling System fitted to the NBCRV version
(© Hans-Hermann Bühling)

The vehicle comes in several variants with a common engine, transmission, hydraulics, wheels, tyres, differentials and transfer case
(© Hans-Hermann Bühling)

The wheels have a ground clearance of 51cm and have Hutchinson 20x8.5 rims
(© Hans-Hermann Bühling)

The tyres are Michelin XML 12.00 R20 steel belt radials with ROF capability
(© Hans-Hermann Bühling)

Commander's hatch (© Hans-Hermann Bühling)

Upper storage racks (© Hans-Hermann Bühling)

The Joint Biological Point Detection System fitted to the Stryker NBCRV
(© Hans-Hermann Bühling)

3 Stryker Profiles

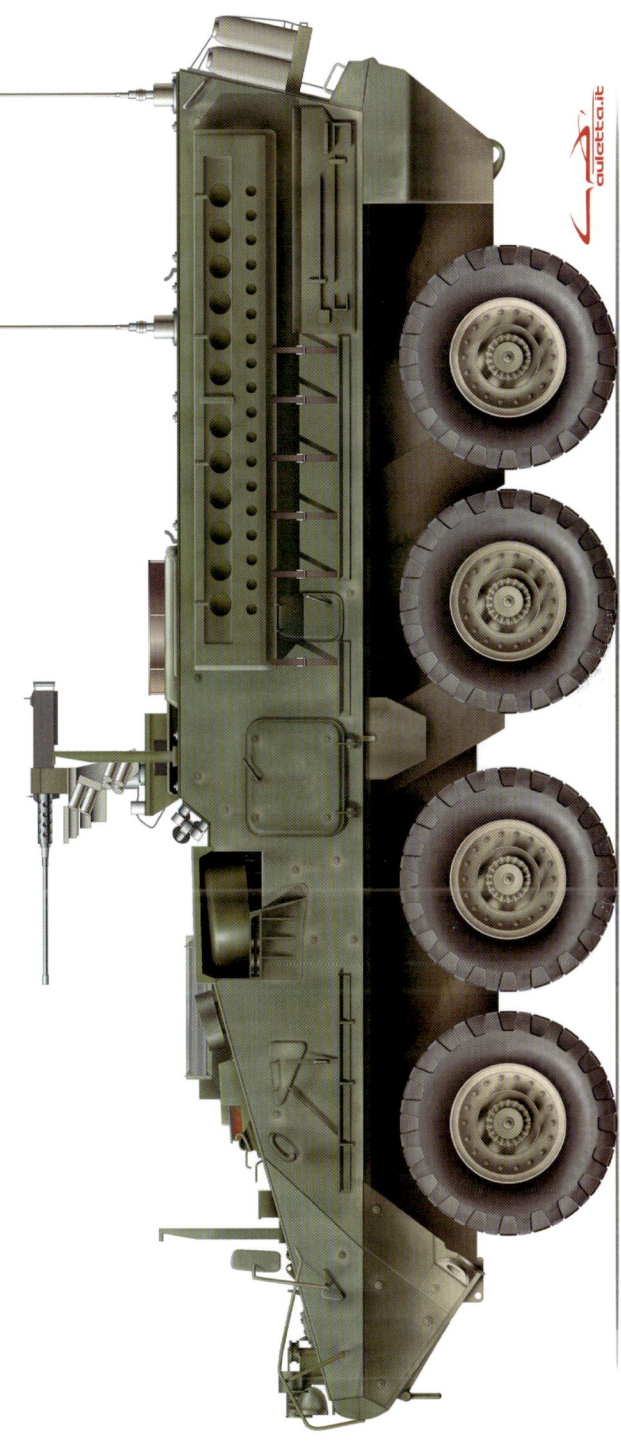

M1126 Stryker Infantry Carrier Vehicle (ICV)
(the slat armour cage is not shown in this drawing)
172nd Stryker Brigade Combat Team
Mosul, Iraq, February 2006

M1126 Stryker Infantry Carrier Vehicle (ICV)
(the slat armour cage is not shown in this drawing)
1-14 Cavalry, 3rd Brigade, SBCT 2nd Infantry Division from Fort Lewis,
Washington, displayed in Iraq to provide security during Operation Block
Party in Mosul, Iraq, in October 2004
The weathering is not heavy

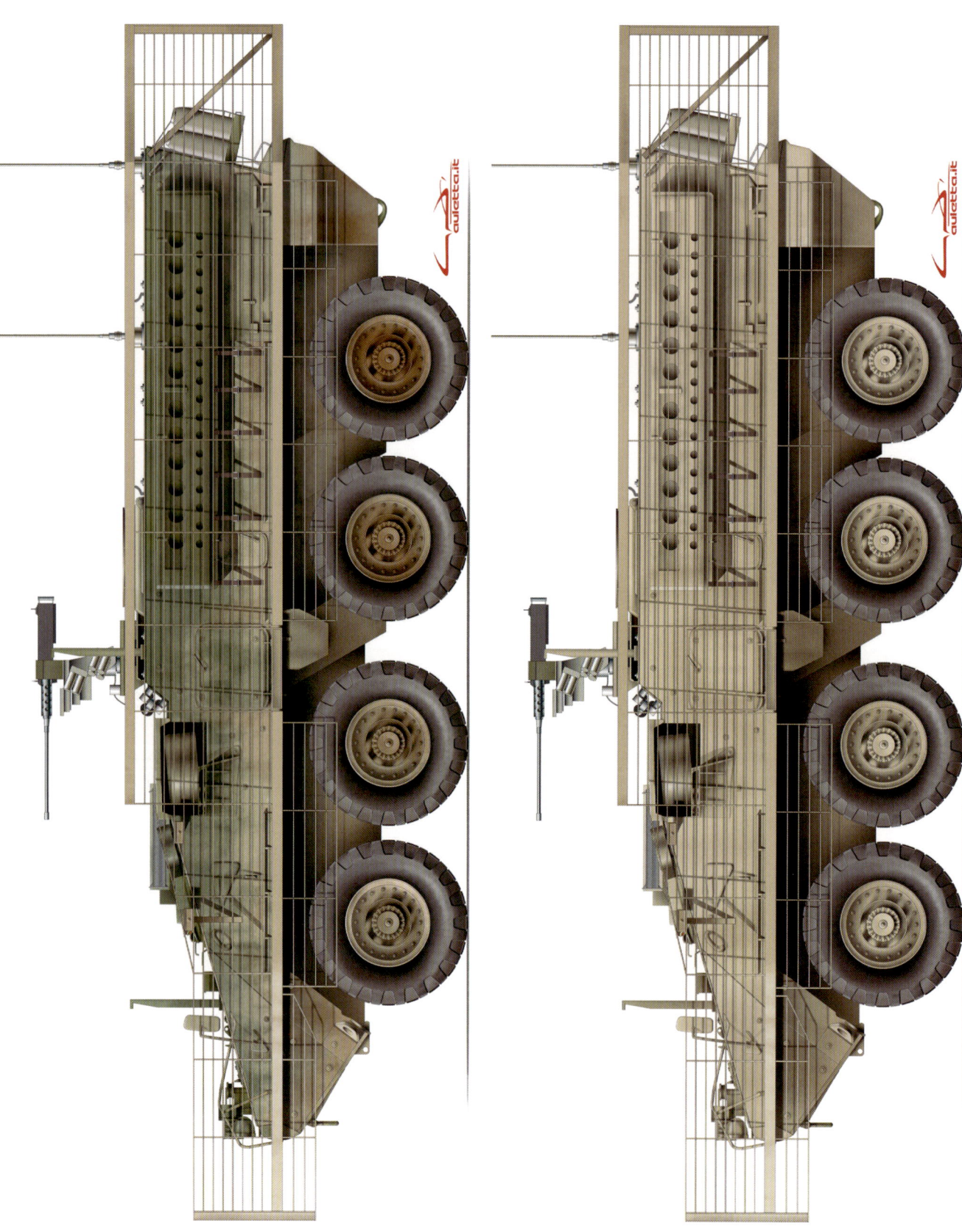

M1126 Stryker Infantry Carrier Vehicle (ICV)
with slat armour cage
Combat Company, 20th Intantry, 3rd Brigade, 2nd Infantry Division
(SBCT), 4th Infantry Division
As it appears during a route reconnaissance and presence patrol
Samarra, Iraq, 15 December 2003

M1126 Stryker Infantry Carrier Vehicle (ICV)
with slat armour cage
2nd Platoon, Bravo Company, 1st Battalion, 5th Infantry Division, Stryker
Brigade Combat Team (SBCT)
Depicted as it appeared during a patrol tour near Mosul, Dahuk, Iraq
Overall desert camouflage

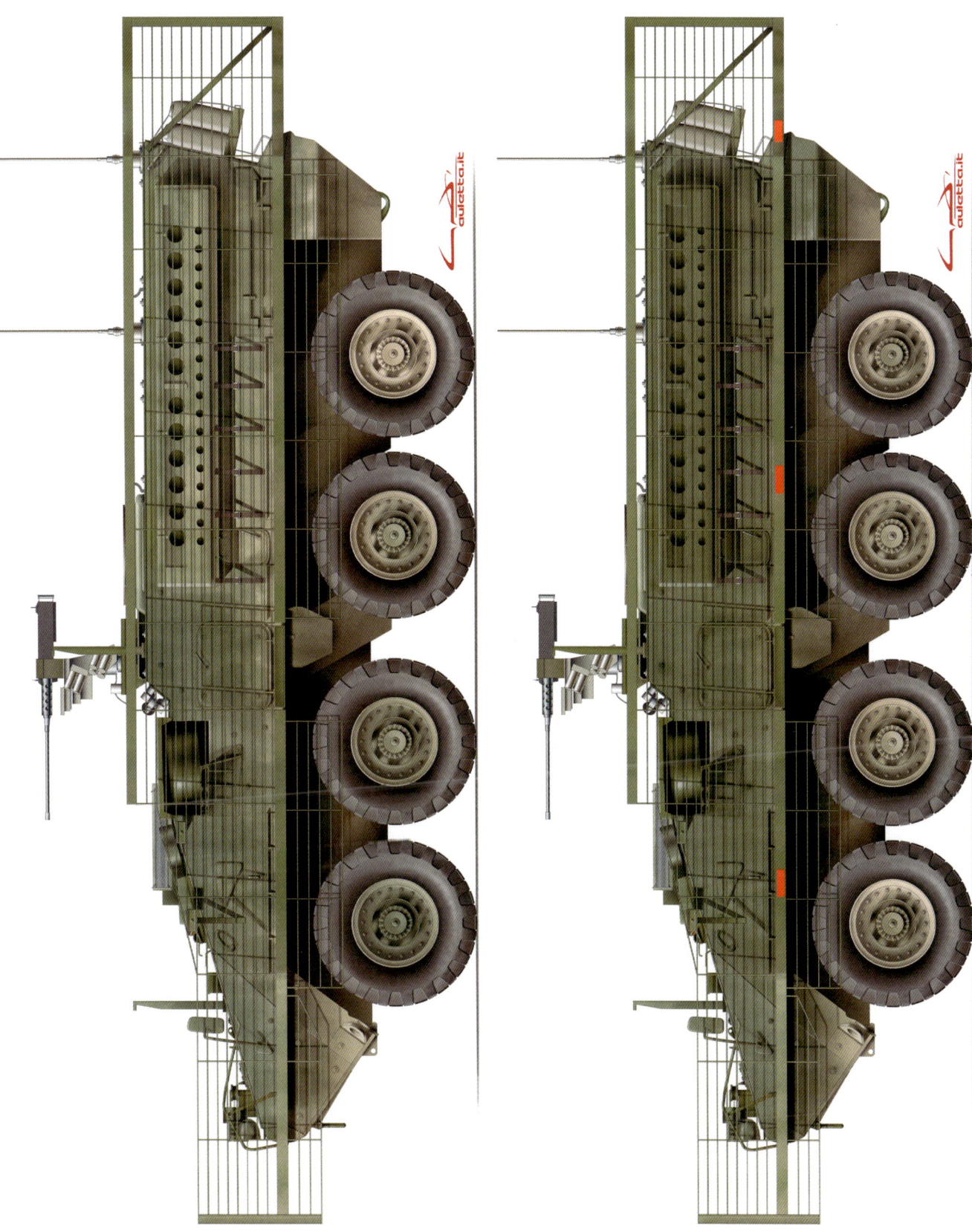

M1126 Stryker Infantry Carrier Vehicle (ICV)
with slat armour cage
Red Platoon, Assassin Company, 414th Brigade, USMC
Rawah City, Al Anbar Province, Iraq, 21 April 2006

M1126 Stryker Infantry Carrier Vehicle (ICV)
with slat armour cage
A Company, 1st Battalion, 38th Infantry Regiment
Iraq, January 2008

3

Modelling the M1126 OIF Stryker

Andy Renshaw

Of all the armored vehicles used in 'Operation Iraqi Freedom', the Stryker is probably one of the most popular subjects. Being such a new vehicle, plastic kit manufacturers had to quickly gather the data, produce tooling, and start producing the entire Stryker family. Trumpeter from China was first on the scene with a decent kit that was quickly purchased by those eager to build the model. AFV Club quickly followed with what is the best Stryker kit on the market, not only is the detail much more crisp, but the overall measurements and shape are far more accurate.

Both Trumpeter and AFV Club have been slowly working their way through the series, each making minor improvements to their previous issues. So far we have the M1126, M1130, and M1134 from both companies. AFV Club has also released a beautiful M1128 MGS kit, and at the time of this writing Trumpeter has released a M1127. I'm sure AFV Club will be quickly following with their own M1127 and conversion sets also exist for the as yet un-kitted M1132 ESV.

So unlike the M2A2 Bradley

and M1A2 Abrams, the base kit needs very little upgrading to bring it to current OIF configuration. However the challenge lies with the fact that the RPG threat has caused all Strykers deployed to Iraq to have 'slat' armour installed. Needless to say, this alone intimidates most modellers away from building a OIF Stryker, as the packages of etch is daunting. However as you can see from the build, taking it a little at a time, step-by-step, none of the construction is beyond the skill of any modeller who has some experience with etch parts.

For this build, we will use the excellent AFV Club offering, along with a few aftermarket additions. The majority of these will be the slat armour, and here we will use the Griffon set. This was chosen because of its completeness, as it comes with everything needed to upgrade the Stryker with slat armour. Other manufacturers also produce slat armour, however they do not come with all the needed armour plates, blast panels, or headlight extensions, and these would all have to be purchased separately. Also the Griffon set uses many different thicknesses of metal, and the slat itself is thick enough to be very close to scale, while remaining manageable in 1:35. The engineering on the kit is also excellent, which helps mitigate some of the challenge and minimise any issues.

One nice thing about this subject is that the Strykers vary greatly, so there are a lot of different ways you can build them beyond the basic slat armour configuration. Some had blast panels, others sandbags and still others had ballistic glass screens added. Stowage varied greatly, as did the weathering. Use the photos in this book and other resources to guide you as you finish your Stryker. So with all that said, let's gather our kits and tools and go to work!

AFV Club's kit of the M1126 is the best on the market. The M1126 is the first Stryker they released, but AFV Club has done several versions since, and has added additional details and improvements with each kit. Many of these can be found in the recently released #35S59 'Upgrade Equipment for Stryker' set

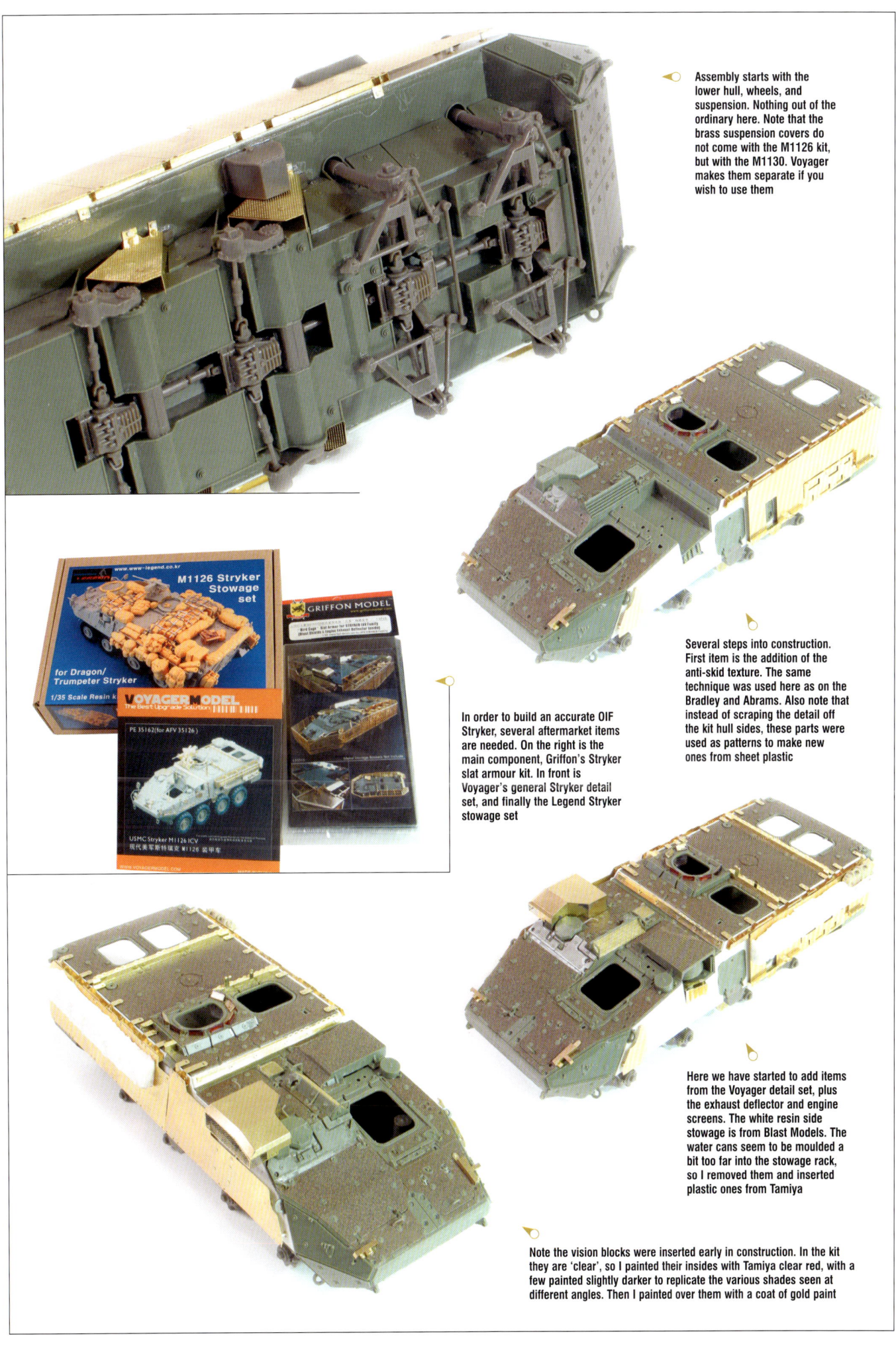

Assembly starts with the lower hull, wheels, and suspension. Nothing out of the ordinary here. Note that the brass suspension covers do not come with the M1126 kit, but with the M1130. Voyager makes them separate if you wish to use them

In order to build an accurate OIF Stryker, several aftermarket items are needed. On the right is the main component, Griffon's Stryker slat armour kit. In front is Voyager's general Stryker detail set, and finally the Legend Stryker stowage set

Several steps into construction. First item is the addition of the anti-skid texture. The same technique was used here as on the Bradley and Abrams. Also note that instead of scraping the detail off the kit hull sides, these parts were used as patterns to make new ones from sheet plastic

Here we have started to add items from the Voyager detail set, plus the exhaust deflector and engine screens. The white resin side stowage is from Blast Models. The water cans seem to be moulded a bit too far into the stowage rack, so I removed them and inserted plastic ones from Tamiya

Note the vision blocks were inserted early in construction. In the kit they are 'clear', so I painted their insides with Tamiya clear red, with a few painted slightly darker to replicate the various shades seen at different angles. Then I painted over them with a coat of gold paint

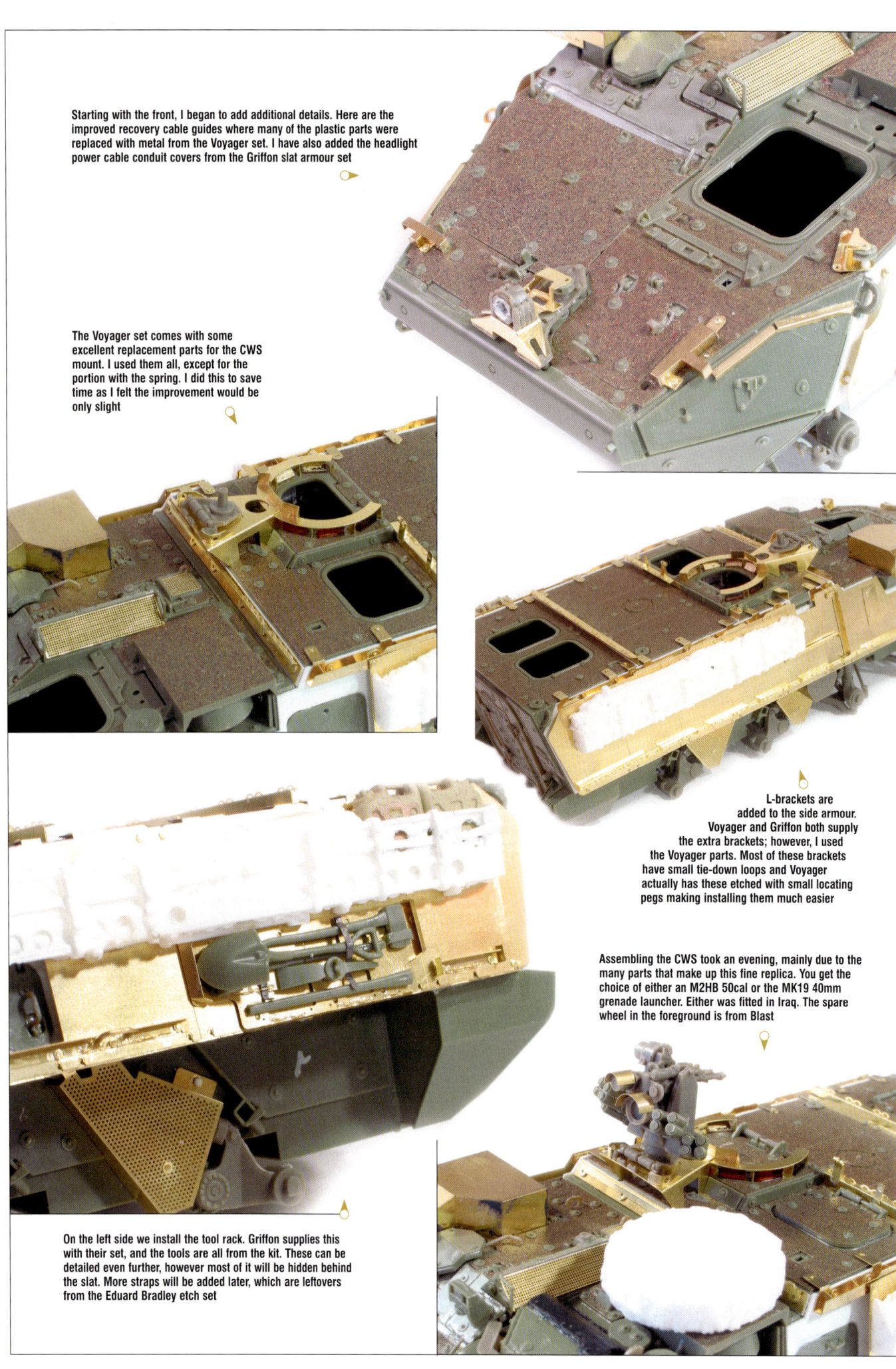

Starting with the front, I began to add additional details. Here are the improved recovery cable guides where many of the plastic parts were replaced with metal from the Voyager set. I have also added the headlight power cable conduit covers from the Griffon slat armour set

The Voyager set comes with some excellent replacement parts for the CWS mount. I used them all, except for the portion with the spring. I did this to save time as I felt the improvement would be only slight

L-brackets are added to the side armour. Voyager and Griffon both supply the extra brackets; however, I used the Voyager parts. Most of these brackets have small tie-down loops and Voyager actually has these etched with small locating pegs making installing them much easier

Assembling the CWS took an evening, mainly due to the many parts that make up this fine replica. You get the choice of either an M2HB 50cal or the MK19 40mm grenade launcher. Either was fitted in Iraq. The spare wheel in the foreground is from Blast

On the left side we install the tool rack. Griffon supplies this with their set, and the tools are all from the kit. These can be detailed even further, however most of it will be hidden behind the slat. More straps will be added later, which are leftovers from the Eduard Bradley etch set

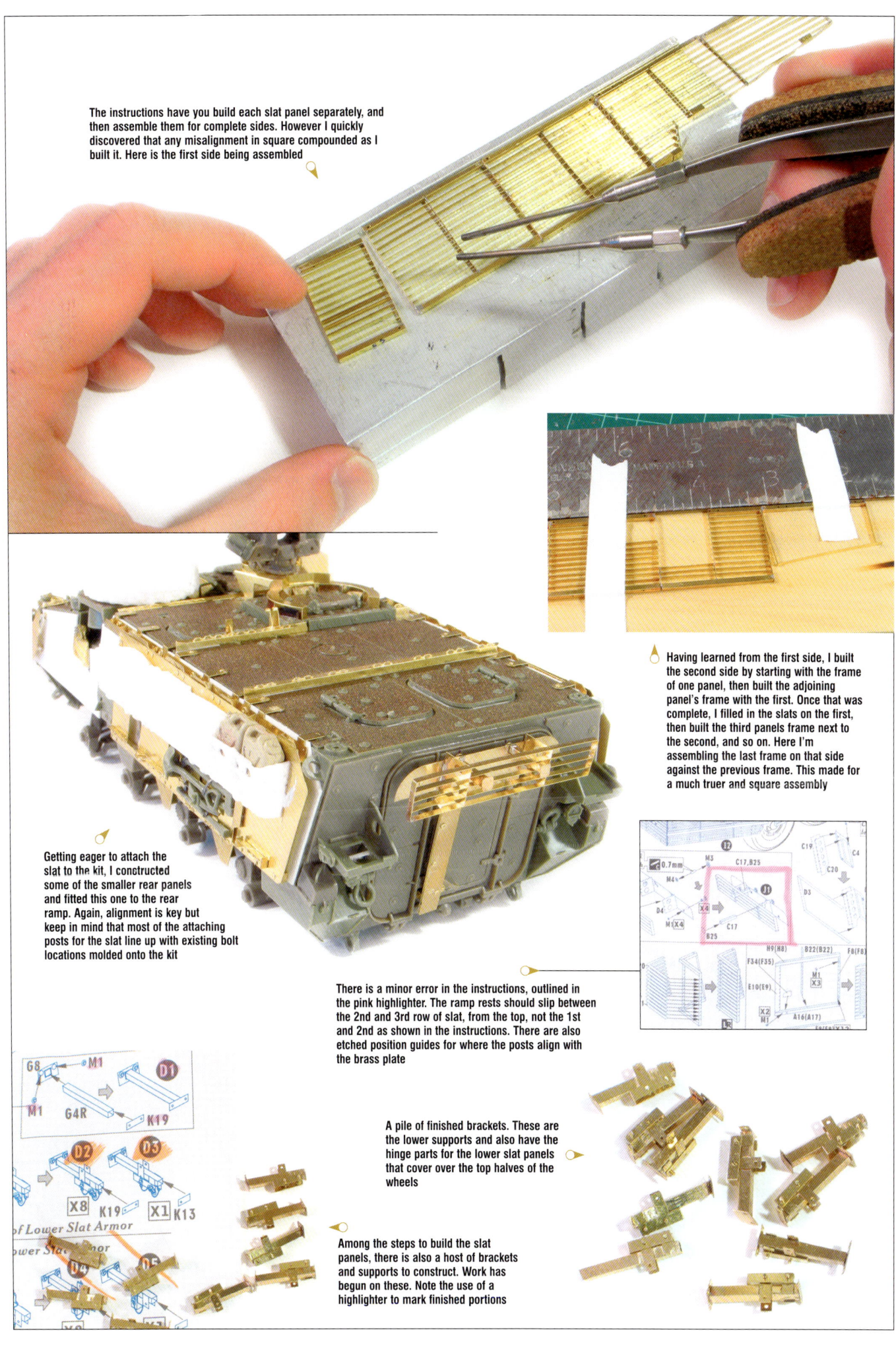

The instructions have you build each slat panel separately, and then assemble them for complete sides. However I quickly discovered that any misalignment in square compounded as I built it. Here is the first side being assembled

Having learned from the first side, I built the second side by starting with the frame of one panel, then built the adjoining panel's frame with the first. Once that was complete, I filled in the slats on the first, then built the third panels frame next to the second, and so on. Here I'm assembling the last frame on that side against the previous frame. This made for a much truer and square assembly

Getting eager to attach the slat to the kit, I constructed some of the smaller rear panels and fitted this one to the rear ramp. Again, alignment is key but keep in mind that most of the attaching posts for the slat line up with existing bolt locations molded onto the kit

There is a minor error in the instructions, outlined in the pink highlighter. The ramp rests should slip between the 2nd and 3rd row of slat, from the top, not the 1st and 2nd as shown in the instructions. There are also etched position guides for where the posts align with the brass plate

A pile of finished brackets. These are the lower supports and also have the hinge parts for the lower slat panels that cover over the top halves of the wheels

Among the steps to build the slat panels, there is also a host of brackets and supports to construct. Work has begun on these. Note the use of a highlighter to mark finished portions

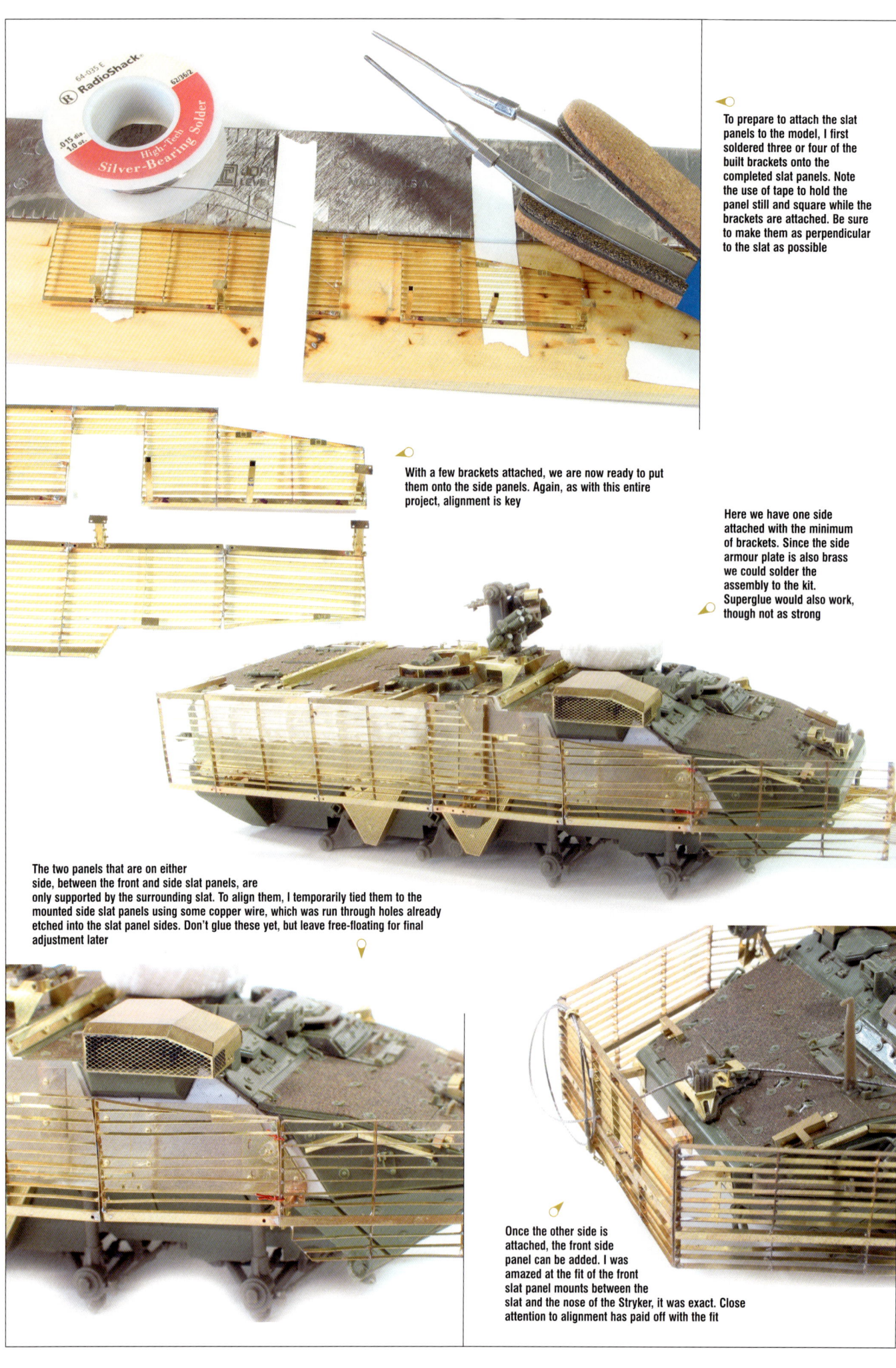

To prepare to attach the slat panels to the model, I first soldered three or four of the built brackets onto the completed slat panels. Note the use of tape to hold the panel still and square while the brackets are attached. Be sure to make them as perpendicular to the slat as possible

With a few brackets attached, we are now ready to put them onto the side panels. Again, as with this entire project, alignment is key

Here we have one side attached with the minimum of brackets. Since the side armour plate is also brass we could solder the assembly to the kit. Superglue would also work, though not as strong

The two panels that are on either side, between the front and side slat panels, are only supported by the surrounding slat. To align them, I temporarily tied them to the mounted side slat panels using some copper wire, which was run through holes already etched into the slat panel sides. Don't glue these yet, but leave free-floating for final adjustment later

Once the other side is attached, the front side panel can be added. I was amazed at the fit of the front slat panel mounts between the slat and the nose of the Stryker, it was exact. Close attention to alignment has paid off with the fit

With both sides now on, plus the front, we can glue the floating slat panels between the front and side slat portions, and add all the remaining mounts. As you can see, some mounts were replaced with square plastic stock the same size as the assembled photo-etch mounts for a better fit. Don't worry about the lower panels, as those will be fitted much later

A look at the lower supports. Note the small retaining chains and pins that are part of the lower bracket assembly. The instructions have you install these while building the brackets, however in order to keep them from getting damaged I waited until after the brackets were installed on the model to attach them

All that is left is the rear. This area is tricky. Don't follow the instructions' order. First assemble the slat panels, keeping them separate. Then assemble the top screen parts and use that as a guide to align the 2 rear panels with the side slat. If you leave the screen portion removable, you can then later insert the water and fuel cans after painting

For a short break, I turned my attention again to the CWS, adding the M2HB 50cal with a extra photo-etched cooling jacket from the spares box, hollowed out the end of the barrel, and some electrical wires for the smoke dischargers. The charging handle (the post sticking out the side of the gun) should be removed, and a solenoid made from scrap plastic rod was added on the right side of the gun. The solenoid allows the gun to be fired electrically vs. manually by the trigger

A shot of the completed rear. At this point the entire slat is done! Note in many of the photos the small bolt etchings (parts M1). I added the bolts in groups, toward the end of the build as the heat from soldering may have had adverse affects on the glue, including releasing various toxic gasses as the glue cured

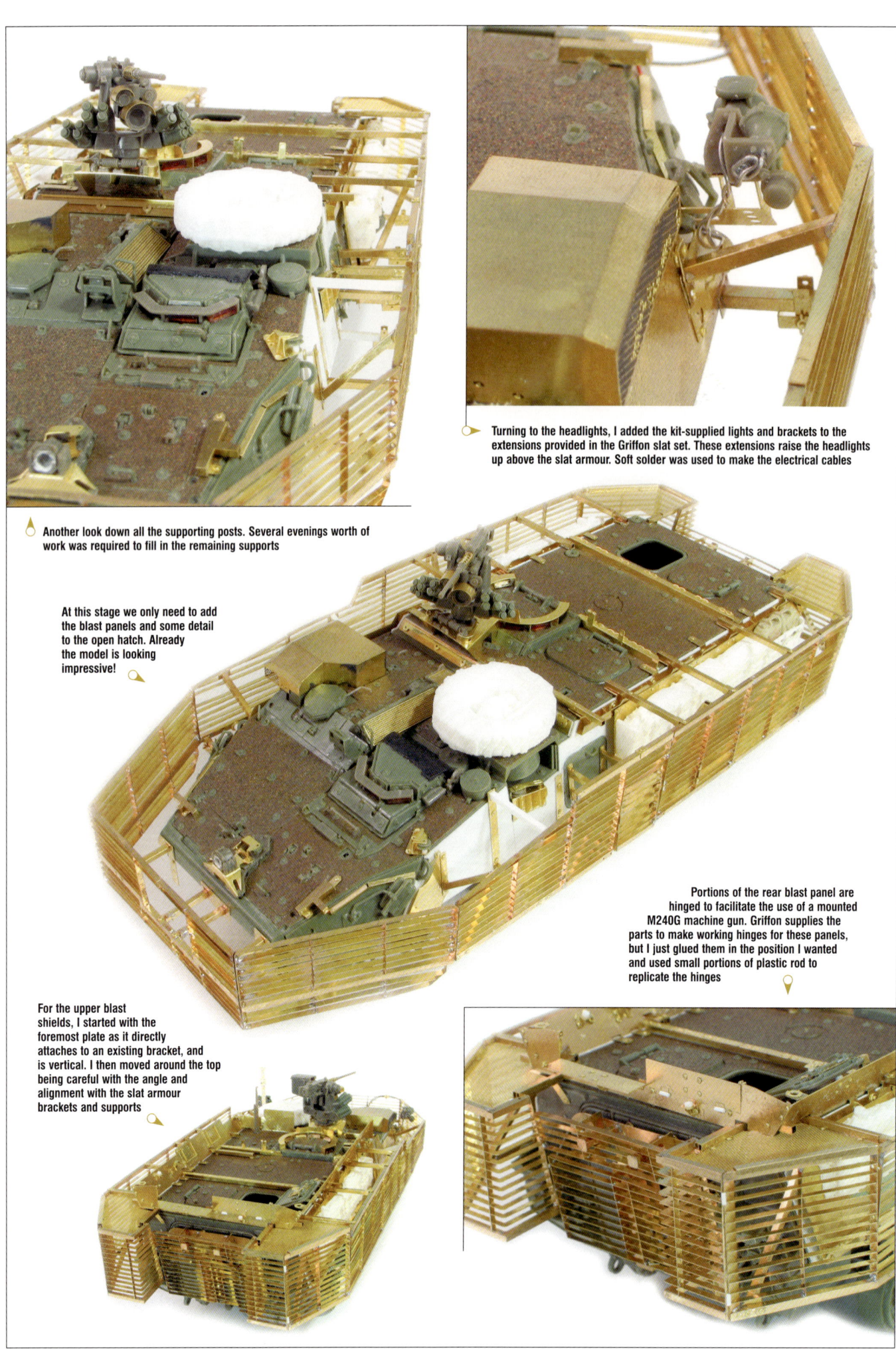

Turning to the headlights, I added the kit-supplied lights and brackets to the extensions provided in the Griffon slat set. These extensions raise the headlights up above the slat armour. Soft solder was used to make the electrical cables

Another look down all the supporting posts. Several evenings worth of work was required to fill in the remaining supports

At this stage we only need to add the blast panels and some detail to the open hatch. Already the model is looking impressive!

Portions of the rear blast panel are hinged to facilitate the use of a mounted M240G machine gun. Griffon supplies the parts to make working hinges for these panels, but I just glued them in the position I wanted and used small portions of plastic rod to replicate the hinges

For the upper blast shields, I started with the foremost plate as it directly attaches to an existing bracket, and is vertical. I then moved around the top being careful with the angle and alignment with the slat armour brackets and supports

Another shot of the rear with the blast panels installed. Notice that I have left off the ventilator housing from the top of the hull. This is because I plan on adding stowage covering this area later

Some photos show the recovery cable extending, and the excess coiled and tied to the front slat armour. The Voyager set provides some beautiful cable to replace the string that comes in the kit. I used the full length, gluing the kit's cable end to the cable, and coiling it up. I also used strips of tape to secure it, and then covered the tape with etched straps

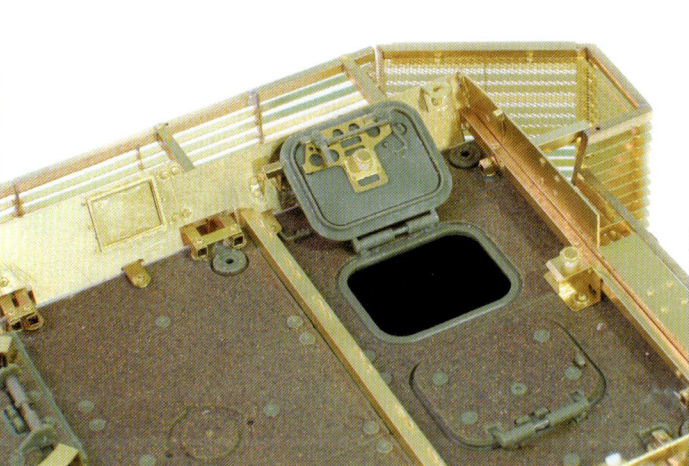

Griffon provides interior details for all the hatches. I chose to use a combination of the photo-etched detail and the kit parts. Numerous bolts cover the interior of the plate, which come with the Griffon set, and each is placed individually

Most vehicles operating later in OIF were provided ECM packages to counter IEDs. One of these was the DUKE system. Legend recently came out with a set of two different ECM antennas, one of which is a DUKE antenna. AFV club later provided this antenna with some of the later Stryker kits, but not with the M1126

A mount for the DUKE antenna was made from plastic sheet and the holes punched with a Waldron punch set. Sharp eyed readers will notice that the spare wheel had to be moved from its previous position. Luckily the superglue didn't hold too tight!

Here is a quick overall shot of the Stryker with the Duke installed. All that is left now is to add some stowage before we begin painting. All that brass is impressive to look at, and it makes for a hefty model

This batch of resin stowage is from the Legend set. It fitted perfectly between the slat armour supports. The net is made from strips of lead foil that is provided in the Legend stowage set, woven through the tie-down loops, and then the cross pattern formed from more strips

A last final shot before we begin painting. Phew, that is a lot of brass, and it does add some weight to the overall model

A special ops night-fighting Stryker? No, just the coat of primer. The 'Rust-Oleum' brand primer was first warmed in hot tap water then sprayed over the entire model. This provides a uniform durable finish that the acrylic base colours can bind to. The dark grey also acts as a wonderful 'pre-shade' to the subsequent painting

Once the primer has dried for twenty-four hours, we can begin painting. For the CARC dark green colour, I used photographs as a reference and created a custom mix of paint to match what I saw. The result was a 50/50 blend of Vallejo Model Air 71006 and 71021, plus a few drops of 70847 to lighten it very slightly. Note I used a sand colour to lighten, not white

Detail painting continues. Careful painting and time spent here will pay off in the long run. By positioning all the resin stowage and painting it with the vehicle, it tends to blend into the overall composition better. Also the dark grey primer makes painting the resin parts much easier. When this is done, an overall coat of 'Johnson's Klear' (Future) prepares the model for the next steps

Before cleaning up the mix used to spray the entire vehicle, a few more drops of sand were added to just lighten the green, and this was then sprayed over the top areas to highlight and to lighten the upper surfaces. Next detail painting of all the gear and parts was done. Tyres were also pressed on after a primer coat of the 'Rust-Oleum' paint

Here is a selection of stowage items not painted with the vehicle, such as the printed accessories. Most of this comes with the Legend Stryker stowage set, including the printed MRE (Meal Ready to Eat) boxes. All of the items get the same treatment as the full size vehicle, including washes and dry brushing. Note that it is easier to paint them when still on the resin plugs, then cut off when ready to use

Allow twenty-four hours for the wash to dry, then dry-brush with a light tan-ish green, or sand colour. I like using oils for this as they blend and offer a much softer tone than enamels or acrylics. Don't use white, as this will make too stark a contrast. You can continue to layer the dry-brushing to get the contrast you desire, and can always add more later to highlight key features. Keeping this subtle is the trick to a realistic finish

The next two steps are washing and dry-brushing, both done with oil paint. The wash is oil thinned with Turpenoid (an odorless thinner) and is mixed 'on the fly' by combining a dab of paint in a small puddle of thinner. This can be done in a plastic lid or a square of tinfoil. This way you can vary the darkness of the wash depending on what you are working over. Also use a very dark brown vs. black, and vary the shade. Run the wash into all crevices and around details

Pigment dust was added to the upper surfaces as well in areas the crew would walk on. Also some rust and yellow ochre coloured pigment was used on the exhaust deflector to replicate the discolouration and rusting effects the hot exhaust has on the thin sheet metal. Again, use photos as a reference

To prepare for final weathering and pigments, some Vallejo Sand was mixed and thinned with water almost 70%. The using an airbrush, a misting of 'dust' was layered on the lower half of the vehicle, keeping reference photos handy at all times!

A close-up after the wash, drybrush, and a flat clear coat to remove the shine from everything. Notice how the details pop out, but are not outlined. This replicates a much more realistic effect of light catching the edge and not an 'outline' effect. However, you can add more if you desire more contrast, as this is an art and each modeller has his own style

The final weathering step is to use pigments to create a good dust and grime effect. Vallejo makes a line of pigments that can be used for a variety of effects. Scoop some pigment into a small dish and add some Turpenoid to make a wash of sorts. Start light, as you can always add more later. Using a wide brush, flow the mixture onto the lower surfaces, and anywhere else dust might collect

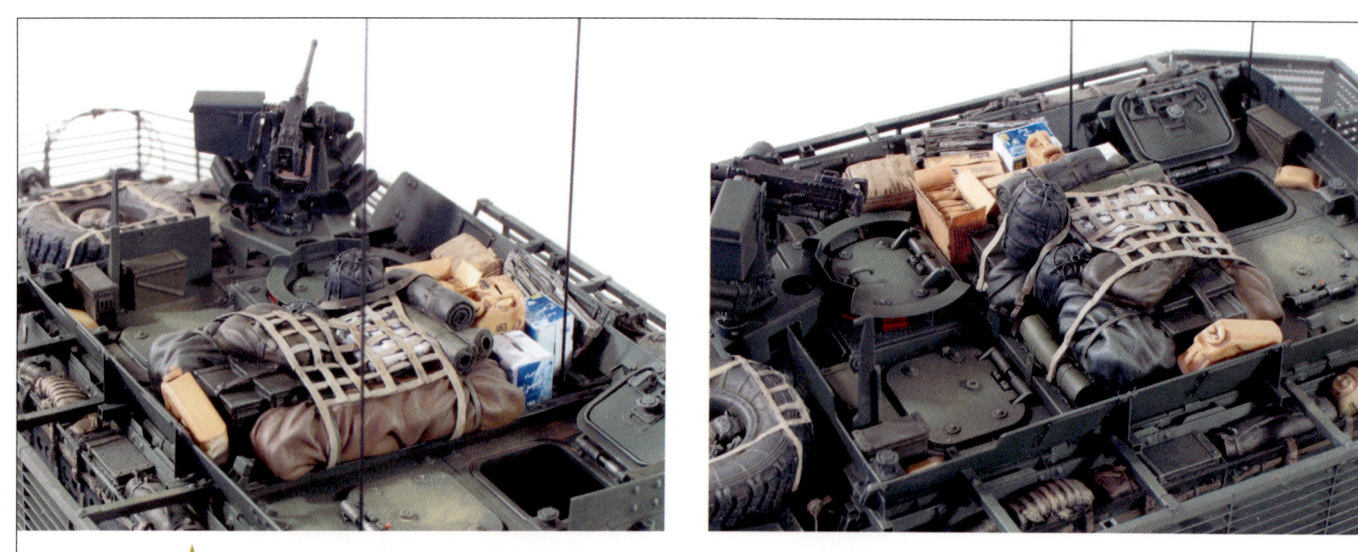

Antennas were made of fine brass wire, cut to a scale 10 foot height. For the tops, I dipped the ends in five-minute epoxy, and then hung the wire upside down. Gravity forms a perfect tear-drop for the top of the antenna

A head-on view showing the coil of barbed wire to good effect

An overall shot. A coil of photo-etched barbed wire has been added to the side. This particular wire came from Verlinden; however more accurate would be some 'razor' wire which is available from Eduard

The additional stowage was added. Use some thought when adding stowed items, as though you are part of the crew. Placement should make sense, as well as be secured or placed in such a way that it wouldn't fall off the vehicle if moving at speed or in rough terrain

The IED Menace

The destruction caused by an Improvised Explosive Device (IED) is evident with the near disintegration of a Cougar

An improvised explosive device or IED, also known as a 'roadside bomb' in contemporary parlance is a homemade device constructed and deployed in ways other than in conventional military action. The term Improvised Explosive Device comes from the British Army in the 1970s, after their experiences with the IRA who used bombs made from agricultural fertilizer and semtex to make highly effective booby trap devices. Currently IEDs designed for use against armored targets such as personnel carriers or tanks will also include some form of armour penetrator, typically consisting of a copper rod or cone, propelled by the shaped explosive load. IEDs are extremely diverse in design, and may contain many types of detonators, penetrators, and explosive packages, and anti-personnel IEDs typically also contain shrapnel-generating objects such as nails or ball bearings and can be triggered by various methods, including remote control, infra-red or magnetic triggers, pressure-sensitive bars or trip wires. In some cases, multiple IEDs are wired together in a 'daisy-chain' to attack a convoy of vehicles spread out along a roadway.

Operation Iraqi Freedom has seen an extensive use of IEDs against coalition forces and they been reported to have been responsible for at least 40% of coalition deaths in Iraq. Common locations for placing these bombs include inside animal carcasses, soft drink cans, boxes or buried inside doorways or passages. Typically they explode underneath or to the side to cause the maximum amount of damage to a vehicle or person; however, as armour has improved on military vehicles, insurgents began placing IEDs in elevated positions such as on road signs, utility poles, or trees, in order to hit less protected areas. IEDs in Iraq were typically made using artillery or mortar shells with varying amounts

A Humvee burns after being hit by a 'roadside bomb'

of bulk or homemade explosives. Early during the Iraq war, the explosives were often obtained from stored munitions bunkers and also by stripping landmines of their explosives. According to the Pentagon, 250,000 tons of Iraqi ordnance has been looted, thus providing a large supply of ammunition for the insurgents.

A Coalition compound littered with the effects of IEDs

A sad end for a Stryker hit, as you can see, from underneath by an IED

Kitography

Abrams Kits

MANUFACTURER	SCALE	REF #	DESCRIPTION	NOTES
Academy	1:35	13202	M1A1 Abrams Iraq 2003	
Dragon	1:35	3536	M1A2 SEP	
Dragon	1/35	3531	M1A1HC	USMC issue
Dragon	1:35	3535	M1A1 AIM	
Italeri	1:35	6438	M1A1 w/ interior	
Italeri	1:35	6390	M1A2	
Revel	1:35	3059	M1A2 Abrams	
Taymia	1:35	35158	M1A1 w/ Mine Plow	
Taymia	1:35	35269	M1A2 Abrams	
Taymia	1:35	35273	M1A1/A2 Photo-etch Details	
Eduard	1:35	35259	M1A2 Abrams	For old DML kit
Eduard	1:35	35333	M1A1 Abrams	For Taymia kit
Eduard	1:35	35806	M1A1 Abrams	For Academy 1345
Eduard	1:35	35510	M1A1 Abrams	For Dragon
Eduard	1:35	35609	M1A2 Abrams	For Italeri
Eduard	1:35	35736	M1A1 Abrams w/ Mine Plow	For Taymia
Eduard	1:35	35806	M1A1 Abrams	For Academy
Eduard	1:35	35807	M1A1 Abrams Iraq 2003	For Academy
Eduard	1:35	35894	M1A1 Abrams	For Italeri 6449
Eduard	1:35	35956	M1A1 Abrams AIM	For Dragon
Eduard	1:35	36006	M1A2 SEP Abrams	For Dragon
Eduard	1:35	B3503	M1A1 Big Ed Set	For Taymia
Eduard	1:35	B3535	M1A1 Big Ed Set	For Dragon
Eduard	1:35	TP013	Zoom M1A1 Abrams	For Taymia
Eduard	1:35	TP072	Zoom M1A2 Abrams	
Eduard	1:35	TP095	M1 120mm Ammo Can	
Legends	1:35	1185	M1A1/M1A2 TUSK Conversion	For Tamiya
Legends	1:35	1177	M1A1/M1A2 TUSK Conversion	For Dragon
Royal Model	1:35	022	M1A1 Detail Set	
Verlinden	1:35	1967	M1A1 Detail Set	For Taymia
Voyager	1:35	35021	M1A2 Abrams Update Set	
Voyager	1:35	35213	M1A2 Reactive Armor Module (TUSK)	
Voyager	1:35	A149	TUSK Slat Armor	
Dragon	1:72	7213	M1A1 w/ Mine Plow	
Dragon	1:72	7215	M1A1 3rd	
Eduard	1/72	22048	M1A1 Detail	
Eduard	1/72	22055	M1A1/ A2 detail	
Revel	1:72	3112	US M1A1 Abrams	
Revel	1:72	3146	M1A2 Stryker	

Markings and Decals for Abrams

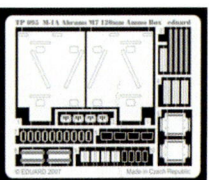

MANUFACTURER	SCALE	REF #	DESCRIPTION	NOTES
Archer	1:35	35190	M1A2 Tank Barrel Slogans	
Archer	1:35	35192	M1A1 3ID/ TF 1-64	
Echelon	1:35	35013	M1A1 HA 3rd ID	
Echelon	1:35	35014	M1A1 HA 3rd ID	
Echelon	1:35	35015	M1A1 HA 3rd ID	
Echelon	1:35	35016	M1A1 HA 3rd ID	
Echelon	1:35	35017	M1A1 HA 4th ID	
Echelon	1:35	35026	M1A1 HC 4th ID	
Echelon	1:35	35031	M1A2 SEP, US Army 4th ID 1st Cav	
Archer	1:72	72190	M1A2 Gun Barrel Slogans	
Archer	1:72	72192	M1A1 3rd ID/ TF 1-64	
Echelon	1:72	72015	M1A1HA OIF part 3	

MANUFACTURER	SCALE	REF #	DESCRIPTION	NOTES
AFV Club	1:35	35012	M1A1 M1A2 Tracks	
Blast	1:35	35057	Bridge Pushing kit	Mostly for USMC abrams
Bronco	1:35	3522	M1A1-M1A2 Workable Tracks	Later type open guide horn
CMK	1:35	3059	M1A1 Engine Set	
Eduard	1:35	35346	M1 Abrams Armor Fittings	For DML
Eduard	1:35	35360	M1 Abrams Armor Fittings	For Tamiya
Eduard	1:35	35590	Exhaust Cover	
Eduard	1:35	35594	M1A1 IFF/CIF ID Panels	
Eduard	1:35	35598	Bustle Rack Extension	
Eduard	1:35	35600	Late Exhaust Cover	
Legends	1:35	1028	M1A1 Engine	
Legends	1:35	1029	M1 Tank Accessories	
Legends	1:35	1163	M1A1 Stowage Set	
Real Model	1:35	35111	M1A1-M1A2 Stowage Set	
Real Model	1:35	35159	M1A2 Stowage Set w/ MOLLE System	
Voyager	1:35	A148	Abrams Side Skirts	For DML
Verlinden	1:35	1964	120mm Ammunition	
Verlinden	1:35	1968	Stowage Set	
Black Dog	1:72	72003	M1A1 Abrams Iraq Stowage and Accessories	
CMK	1:72	V064	M1A1 Equipment Set	
Legends	1:72	7207	M1 Stowage Set	

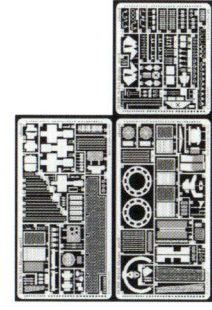

MANUFACTURER	SCALE	REF #	DESCRIPTION	NOTES
Tamiya	1:35	35264	M2A2 Bradley ODS	
Academy	1:35	13205	M2A2 Bradley OIF Iraq 2003	
Blast	1:35	35065K	ERA Armor for M2A2	
Eduard	1:35	35583	M2 Bradley Interior	
Eduard	1:35	35583	M2 Bradley Interior	
Eduard	1:35	35584	M2 Bradley Exterior	
Eduard	1:35	35613	M2 Bradley Turret Interior	
Eduard	1:35	35781	M2A2 Bradley IFV	
Eduard	1:35	35920	M2A2 Bradley OIF	Academy kit
Eduard	1:35	36004	M2 Bradley Stowage Boxes	
Legend	1:35	1189	M2A2-M2A3 Detail Set	
Legend	1:35	1175	M2A3 w/ ERA Conversion	
Legend	1:35	1168	M2A2 ERA Set	
Legend	1:35	1170	M2A3 Bradley Conversion	
Dragon	1:72	7298	M2A2 Bradley w/ ERA	
Dragon	1:72	7229	M3A2 Bradley ODS	
Trumpeter	1:72	7295	M2 Bradley	
Trumpeter	1:72	7297	M2A2 ODS Bradley	
Extratech	1:72	72040	M2A2 Detail Set	For Revell
Extratech	1:72	72041	M2A2 Armor Plates	For Revell
Part	1:72	72088	M2A2 Detail Set	For Revell

MANUFACTURER	SCALE	REF #	DESCRIPTION	NOTES
AFV Club	1:35	35133	Bradley Workable Track, Late Type	
Barrel Depot	1:35	35022	25mm Bushmaster Barrel	
Barrel Depot	1:35	35050	25mm Bushmaster Barrel, Fluted	
Blast	1:35	35023K	M2/M3 Bradley Running Gear with Late Style Track	
Eduard	1:35	TP038	M2A2 Bradley Baggage Ties	
Friulmodel	1:35	ATL78	M2/M3/MLRS/AAVP Track Early Type	Comes with sprocket
Friulmodel	1:35	ATL79	M2/M3/MLRS/AAVP Track Late Type	Comes with sprocket
Legends	1:35	1182	M2 Bradley Road Wheel Set	Also suitable for MLRS, AAVP-7 RAM/RS
Legends	1:35	1119	Bradley Stowage Set	
Verlinden	1:35	1969	Stowage Set	
Real Model	1:35	35038	Engine Set for Bradley	
Real Model	1:35	35141	M2A2 Stowage Set w/ PE Side Racks	
Black Dog	1:72	72006	M2 Bradley Stowage and Accessories	
Legend	1:72	7203	M2 Bradley Stowage and Accessories	
Legend Club	1:72	7205	M2A2 Bradley OIF stowage	

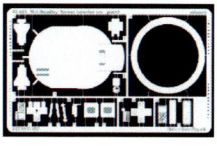

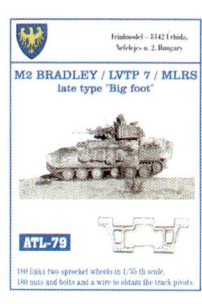

M1126 ICV
Stryker Kits

MANUFACTURER	SCALE	REF #	DESCRIPTION	NOTES
AFV Club	1:35	AF35126	M1126 Stryker	Highly detailed and accurate
Trumpeter	1:35	35375	M1126 Stryker ICV	
Black Dog	1:35	35001	M1126 Interior	For AFV Club
Eduard	1:35	35982	M1126 Stryker Detail Set	For Trumpeter
Eduard	1:35	35991	M1126 Mounted Rack and Belts	For Trumpeter
Eduard	1:35	35993	M1126 Stryker ICV Details Set	For AFV Club
Eduard	1:35	35995	Stryker Slat Armor	For Trumpeter
Eduard	1:35	36001	Stryker Additional Belts	
Eduard	1:35	36002	Stryker Slat Armor	For AFV Club
Eduard	1:35	36003	M1126 Mounted Rack and Belts	For AFV Club
Eduard	1:35	36011	Additional Armor Plates	For AFV Club
Eduard	1:35	36015	Additional Armor Plates	For Trumpeter
Eduard	1:35	36017	Stryker Blast Panels	For AFV Club
Eduard	1:35	36033	Stryker Blast Panels	For Trumpeter
Eduard	1:35	B3548	Big Ed M1126 Detail Set	For AFV Club
Eduard	1:35	B3549	Big Ed M1126 Detail Set	For Trumpeter
Griffon	1:35	L35012	M1126 Detail Set w/ Metal MK19 Barrel	For AFV Club
Griffon	1:35	L35013	Slat Armor w/ Blast Panels and Armor	For AFV Club
Griffon	1:35	L35014	Stowage Baskets for Strykers	For AFV Club
ProArt Models	1:35	35026	Slat Armor for Stryker	Resin and Photo etched
Trumpeter	1:35	06603	M1126 Stryker Upgrade Set	For Trumpeter
Voyager	1:35	35142	M1126 Detail w/ Resin Wheels	For Trumpeter
Voyager	1:35	35162	M1126 Detail Set	For AFV Club
Voyager	1:35	35200	Stryker M1126 Slat Armor	For AFV Club
Voyager	1:35	A100	M1126 Slat Armor	For AFV Club
Voyager	1:35	A116	Spaced Armor for M1126	For AFV Club
Trumpeter	1:72	7255	M1126 Stryker ICV	
Academy	1:72	13411	M1126 Stryker ICV	
Eduard	1:72	22127	M1126 Stryker Detail Set	For Trumpeter
Eduard	1:72	22129	M1126 Stryker Slat Armor	

M1127 RV
Stryker Kits

MANUFACTURER	SCALE	REF #	DESCRIPTION	NOTES
Trumpeter	1:35	35395	M1127 Stryker RV	
Eduard	1:35	36061	M1127 Stryker RV Detail Set	For Trumpeter
Eduard	1:35	36063	M1127 Mounted Rack and Belts	For Trumpeter
Eduard	1:35	36091	M1127 Stowage Belts	For AFV Club
Real Model	1:35	35121	M1127 Stryker Recon Vehicle Conversion	Conversion for AFV Club Stryker kit
Real Model	1:35	35122	M1127 Conversion w/ Slat Armor	Conversion for AFV Club
Real Model	1:35	35124	M1127 Conversion w/ Slat Armors, Blast Panels, Rhino Anti-IED Device	Conversion for AFV Club

M1128 MGS
Stryker Kits

MANUFACTURER	SCALE	REF #	DESCRIPTION	NOTES
AFV Club	1:35	AF35128	M1128 Stryker MGS	
Eduard	1:35	36018	M1130 Stryker CV Detail Set	For AFV Club
Eduard	1:35	36023	M1130 Mounted Rack and Belts	For AFV Club
Eduard	1:35	36025	Stryker Slat Armor	For AFV Club
Eduard	1:35	36026	Additional Armor Plates	For AFV Club
Eduard	1:35	36033	Stryker Blast Panels	For Trumpeter
Eduard	1:35	B3551	Big Ed M1130 Detail Set	For AFV Club

M1130 CV
Stryker Kits

MANUFACTURER	SCALE	REF #	DESCRIPTION	NOTES
AFV Club	1:35	AF35130	M1130 Stryker CV	
Trumpeter	1:35	35397	M1130 Stryker CV	
Eduard	1:35	36018	M1130 Stryker CV Detail Set	For AFV Club
Eduard	1:35	36023	M1130 Mounted Rack and Belts	For AFV Club
Eduard	1:35	36025	Stryker Slat Armor	For AFV Club
Eduard	1:35	36026	Additional Armor Plates	For AFV Club
Eduard	1:35	36033	Stryker Blast Panels	For Trumpeter
Eduard	1:35	36092	M1130 Stowage Belts	For AFV Club
Eduard	1:35	B3551	Big Ed M1130 Detail Set	For AFV Club
Voyager	1:35	35188	M1130 Detail Set	For AFV Club

MANUFACTURER	SCALE	REF #	DESCRIPTION	NOTES
Blast Models	1:35	35139K	M1132 Conversion w/ Vee Blade Surface Mine Plow	

MANUFACTURER	SCALE	REF #	DESCRIPTION	NOTES
AFV Club	1:35	AF35134	M1134 Stryker ATGM	
Trumpeter	1:35	35399	M1134 Stryker ATGM	
Eduard	1:35	36018	M1130 Stryker CV Detail Set	For AFV Club
Eduard	1:35	36023	M1130 Mounted Rack and Belts	For AFV Club
Eduard	1:35	36025	Stryker Slat Armor	For AFV Club
Eduard	1:35	36026	Additional Armor Plates	For AFV Club
Eduard	1:35	36033	Stryker Blast Panels	For Trumpeter
Eduard	1:35	B3551	Big Ed M1130 Detail Set	For AFV Club

MANUFACTURER	SCALE	REF #	DESCRIPTION	NOTES
AFV Club	1:35	AF35157	M151 Remote Weapon Station	Also suitable for M1A1 TUSK concept
AFV Club	1:35	AF35S59	Upgrade Equipment for Stryker	
AFV Club	1:35	AFTH35006	Etching Parts, Intake Mesh, etc	For AFV Club kits
Blast Models	1:35	35114K	Stowage Set #1	For AFV Club
Blast Models	1:35	35115K	Stowage Set #2	
Blast Models	1:35	35146K	US M151 RWS Version A2	
Blast Models	1:35	35134K	Improvised Obstacle Blade for Stryker	
Eduard	1:35	TP087	Exhaust Deflector	For AFV Club
Eduard	1:35	TP096	Exhaust Deflector	For Trumpeter
Eduard	1:35	TP097	Rhino Anti IED Device	
D-Toys	1:35	35004	Stryker 'Infra-red detection' Wheels	For AFV Club
Legends	1:35	1153	Stowage Set	
ProArt Models	1:35	35008	Equipment Set for Strykers	Tow bars, spent round basket, exhaust deflector, other details
ProArt Models	1:35	35027	Sagged Tyres for Stryker	For AFV Club
Real Model	1:35	35208	Drivers Enhancement Kit	For AFV Club, additional mine protection
Real Model	1:35	35138	Stryker Stowage Set #1	
Real Model	1:35	35149	M1126 Stowage Set #2 MOLLE System	
Real Model	1:35	35143	Stryker Wheels	For AFV Club
Real Model	1:35	35151	Stryker Wheels	For Trumpeter
Real Model	1:35	35153	Stryker Signs OIF	printed
Real Model	1:35	35180	Rhino Anti IED Device	
Trumpeter	1:35	06611	LAV III/ Stryker Windscreen	
Voyager	1:35	A094	Stryker Wheels	For Trumpeter
Voyager	1:35	A095	Suspension Cover	
Voyager	1:35	A096	OVM and Water/Fuel Can for Stryker	
Voyager	1:35	A097	Fastening Bolts for Stryker	
Voyager	1:35	A167	Modern US Army Woven Strap	
Voyager	1:35	A169	Modern US Stryker Family Antenna Set	
Black Dog	1:72	72002	Stryker Stowage and Accessories	
D-Toys	1:72	72001	Stryker Wheels	
Legends	1:72	7208	Stowage Set	

M1132 ESV Stryker Kits

M1134 ATGM Stryker Kits

Miscellaneous for all Strykers

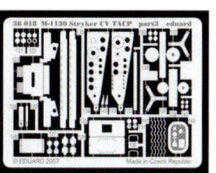

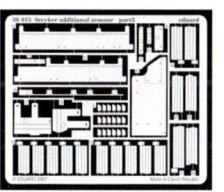

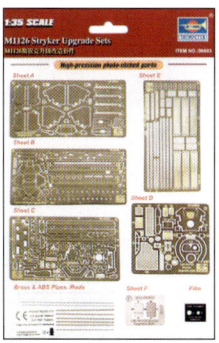

The end of a long day for this Abrams and its crew as the desert night falls